Alistaire & Marie, Phil. 1:3-6

In Jesus,

Charles & Verna

†††

The Church
I Couldn't Find

How a First Century Church May
Look in the 21st Century

Charles Alexander

WestBow
PRESS
A DIVISION OF THOMAS NELSON

WestBow Press books may be ordered through booksellers or by contacting:

WestBow Press
A Division of Thomas Nelson
1663 Liberty Drive
Bloomington, IN 47403
www.westbowpress.com
1-(866) 928-1240

Because of the dynamic nature of the Internet, any web addresses or links contained in this book may have changed since publication and may no longer be valid. The views expressed in this work are solely those of the author and do not necessarily reflect the views of the publisher, and the publisher hereby disclaims any responsibility for them.

Any people depicted in stock imagery provided by Thinkstock are models, and such images are being used for illustrative purposes only.
Certain stock imagery © Thinkstock.

Some of the material in this book is revised substance from my former book, There Must Be Another Way.

Scriptures taken from the Holy Bible, New International Version®, NIV®. Copyright © 1973, 1978, 1984, 2011 by Biblica, Inc.™ Used by permission of Zondervan. All rights reserved worldwide. www.zondervan.com The "NIV" and "New International Version" are trademarks registered in the United States Patent and Trademark Office by Biblica, Inc.™ All rights reserved.

New Revised Standard Version Bible, copyright 1989, Division of Christian Education of the National Council of the Churches of Christ in the United States of America. Used by permission. All rights reserved.

ISBN: 978-1-4497-8943-5 (sc)
ISBN: 978-1-4497-8942-8 (hc)
ISBN: 978-1-4497-8944-2 (e)
Library of Congress Control Number: 2013905434
Printed in the United States of America.
WestBow Press rev. date: 8/1/2013

For resources to enable discipleship and the developing of ministry principles outlined in this book, please see Charles Alexander's Timothy Institute Resources Society web page: www.timothyministry.ca.

CONTENTS

Acknowledgments

I am thankful to God for the prayers and support of my beautiful wife, Verna. She was wonderfully supportive in our joint search. Thank you to our fabulous GenX family, Kara, Leah, and Mark for their helpful input and suggestions regarding the latest draft of this book. Thank you to my longtime friend, Pastor John Briscall, for his gift of encouragement and for his useful suggestions. I am also grateful to Pastor Ron Cooker for reminding me that this book is intended for ordinary and enthusiastic church leaders.

CHAPTER 1

Why Were We Looking?

"*W*here shall we go tomorrow, love?"

"I don't know anymore," Verna often replied.

It was always a Saturday night when we asked that question of each other. We spent well over a year asking the same question, pondering week after week where we were going to worship the next day. After every church service, after reading each church bulletin and after asking a lot of questions, Verna and I offered each other the same hesitant look. We shrugged our shoulders a lot. We'd stayed loyal to our lifelong denomination for years, sure that our vision for a Second Reformation church must be found somewhere. Peter Wagner describes this growing attitude as the New Apostolic Reformation movement "in which the character of these churches are developing around new paradigms."[1]

After spending most of my working life as a pastor in the Anglican church of Canada, I retired early. It's not that I gave up. Indeed, much of my ministry turned out to be of a prophetic nature. The revisionist forces in mainline churches were hard at work. To make a long story short, there were a lot of people who wanted a different kind of church

---

1   Peter C. Wagner, *Churchquake.* (Ventura, CA: Regal Books, 1999), 33.

than the one left behind by the twelve apostles. Quite deliberately, I did more than my fair share in helping to remedy that situation.

Having been graciously affirmed in an apostolic ministry by the people of St. James' Church in Calgary, Alberta, I had been very busy. For more than twenty years, I spent about two Sundays of every month away from the church. I engaged in church and clergy conferences wherever I was requested.

Just before I entered the task of building a new church at the embryonic community of St. James, I came into a further experience of God. It was something, though not quite the same as John Wesley's *Second Blessing.* The experience was known as the baptism of the Holy Spirit. I'll speak of it some more later.

After a few years at this rapidly growing church in suburban Calgary, and after cofounding the Anglican Renewal movement with John Vickers of Victoria, I began accepting invitations to conduct conferences. At my next charge in Metchosin, Victoria, they also agreed to let me continue in this ministry. My congregation seemed to be very happy when I worked for God somewhere else.

I spent all those years teaching in every region of Canada, in many parts of the United States, and in a variety of places throughout the world. God was doing a "new thing" (Isa. 43:18–19). He was changing many lives through this Charismatic Renewal Movement. But changed people are never satisfied with the status quo—not if there are better ways to achieve kingdom purposes.

In those conferences, people were challenged to look into new priorities and different ways of doing church. People were excited; the Jesus of history was really alive! They knew Him to be the head of the church in real terms. He inspired them to reexamine how to accomplish the main purposes of His community. I didn't know it, but in those early days of renewal, we were on the edge of a second reformation.

That was all very good, of course, but I was getting frustrated. The system allowed for this burst of new spirituality, and that was all right with the hierarchical powers, provided that *those people* didn't try to force open the bottleneck in the system. The fact is the entire structures of the church needed renewal. The old system actually hindered the effective renewal of the church, from top to bottom. (Actually, these systemic problems also existed in almost every other church denomination.)

Not surprisingly, the revisionists of mainline churches were the most vocal in their protests. Of course they were; the hierarchical positions that bottled up the free flow of God's people also provided a perfect vehicle for controlling the church and executing their own revisionist agendas.

In protest, a number of mainline groups from a variety of denominations grew restless. By this time, we were approaching the beginning of the twenty-first century. For about thirty years, the Charismatic Movement had extended its arms of love into the far reaches of the church. Not everyone understood it. Some thought renewal was all about raising hands or singing with guitars. The renewal was about much more than individual spirituality or the raising of hands to the rhythm of a guitar. It had a lot of social implications, both within and outside of church life. At the turn of the century, and in some of the mainline churches, separation from the parent bodies began to occur. Through slow and deliberate deviousness, the authority of the Bible was being eroded.

It's not that many mainline members were fundamentalists—I, for one, am not—but most of us love the Scripture and would defend the Bible's authority with our very last breath. Actually, I am able to use the word *infallibility*, but in a different way than my fundamentalist brethren:

> The Bible records the infallible purposes of God in His
> work of creation, redemption, and restoration.

Unfortunately, many people grew up to be quite ignorant of the depth and importance of the Bible. Many could not defend the historical faith on the basis of substantive biblical authority. However, revisionists rarely faced issues on the basis of the historical faith but rather on the basis of contemporary sentimentality. It was expressed in attitudes such as, "How do I feel about that?" or "Does it make me uncomfortable?" or "There is no absolute truth" and "My truth is as good as yours." In me-centered cultures, it was, "What does it do for me?" And in churches where historical and biblical authority had been supplanted by the forces of democracy, revisionists were slowly securing their own agendas. The egoism of Eden was finding a new playing field. The historic faith was slowly being eroded by means of the democratic vote. The entire process reminded me of that interesting passage in Daniel.

> He shall speak words against the Most High, shall wear out the holy ones of the Most High, and shall attempt to change the sacred seasons and the law. (Dan.7:25 NRSV)

I, as one whose articles were sometimes censored before they were printed in my denominational newspaper, realized that revisionists controlled the flow of information to the general populace. I was not popular with some centralized authorities when I challenged them privately and publicly, particularly concerning issues that were clearly addressed in the New Testament.

Second, there were too many leaders who doubted Jesus Christ to be, universally, the Lord for the whole world. Nevertheless, many of us tenaciously defended the apostolic position that Jesus is *the* Way, *the* Truth, and *the* Life (John 14:6). Not only did we believe it, but we were also able to thoughtfully articulate that Jesus Christ is unique. He is both God and human. It was God Himself who offered Himself for love of all His creation. In revisionist thinking, Jesus was just one of many pathways on a mythical mountain leading upward to God.

Unfortunately, many of the purveyors of such apostasy appeared to be experientially ignorant of the real story. Indeed, all too many leaders appeared to lack personal experience with God's salvation chronicle. They didn't seem to know that the story of salvation was exactly the reverse of all religious stories on this mountain. For many, religion was analogous to a mountain with many pathways leading up to God. But the Christian story is precisely the reverse of this fanciful notion. It's about God, who has come down from the mountain and has met us at the bottom, where we are. That is, humanity is in a position where God could not be reached through religious activity, through prayer, through being nice, or through any self-effort.

He came down to us because we could no longer reach up to Him. When a religious pathway supposedly led to God, what kind of a deity were people finding up there? In reality, the deities of religions take their place in a long list of mutual contradictions. (For example, not all religions even include a belief in God. In Monist thought, Buddhists don't have a God at all; everything is one.) So in the vast array of religious thought, it is not surprising that there are many contradictions.

Third, this apostasy came to a ruthless head in an arena where many did not want to be challenged or disturbed. The secular view of human sexuality widely insinuated itself in almost every branch of church life and council discussion. At a time when creation theology was almost extinct, God's purposes for sexuality met the deaf ears of a me-centered and feely generation. Many mainline churches, including my own, obscenely courted the favor of the world by asking the culture what the church could bless next. The cry of Jeremiah was constantly burst upon our ears.

> Are they ashamed of their loathsome conduct? No, they have no shame at all; they do not even know how to blush. (Jer. 6:15)

> Truth has perished; it has vanished from their lips. (Jer. 7:28)

It was no accident of time that many apostate people found themselves in significant seats of power. Of course, the ongoing battles were conducted in predictable directions. They were very rarely engaged in debate tested on the basis of biblical and historical substance. After all, the current values of culture were being borne on the wings of sentimental *me-ism*.

What I mean by sentiment is that the forces of revisionism would not be tested through historical and biblical substance. Discussion was always channeled through communal feelings, the individualism of what is good for me, and the bigotry of relaying the message that, if you do not agree with me, then you must be a very intolerant person. "I am so inclusive in my thinking, so you are the one who must be bigoted." Many uninformed people called upon to be decision-makers were not difficult targets. Political manipulators found easy agreement to their agendas. It is often seen to be successful through middle-class, middle-aged, insecure people. It hasn't been difficult to exploit this very large field with, "How can you disagree with our very generous, unbigoted view and not see yourself as being intolerant?"

I began to see the earlier and more traditional seeds of intolerance in my first year at college in Canada. Through an extraordinary process of God's revelation, I accepted His call to study for ordination in Canada. My way had been cleared to do my seminary work in England, but God's leading prevailed. In September 1961, I found myself engaged in first-year studies at Emmanuel College, Saskatoon (in the Saskatchewan, Prairie region of Canada). As a young boy, I grew up in Liverpool during the blitzes and witnessed the death of my two cousins in the street and many neighbors across from our own house. Nevertheless, I count that first year in college as the worst year of my entire life. I became a victim of the reverse cultural coziness that paralyzed the age.

Never in my entire life had I found it difficult to make friends, but that first year in Canada was probably the loneliest year of my life. I befriended a student who was a homosexual. (From clear biblical perspectives, God does not bless homosexual activity, but He loves all people and calls all of us to a relationship through repentance.) Actually, we had made a very casual acquaintance while I was a student at Church Army College in London, England. This young man had previously been a graduate of that college. I never did graduate! After a year of flouting too many Victorian house rules, this former street fighter was asked, "For the sake of the discipline of the college, please don't come back."

It really was a pity that the Church Army could not take this rebel and unpolished diamond from Liverpool and quietly shape him into what was something that was at least nearly acceptable to the system. I must say that many years later, after being the guest speaker at the annual Church Army Canadian conference, Captain Walter Marshal (the head of Church Army in Canada) proposed that I be made an honorary graduate of the organization. I am grateful to God for His humor and my long-time relationship with Church Army. I am officially a Church Army captain! Now let's get back to Emmanuel College.

By association, many of the students assumed I was also homosexual. I was stunned! For the first time in my life, I was lonely. It is interesting that many of those students who shunned friendship with me later became advocates of the homosexual agenda. I became a *leper* once more. Isn't it strange? Previously those who shunned me were being true to the culture of the day. Many years later, they had reversed their position but remained true to the culture of a succeeding generation. In all times, hopefully, I remained true to the gospel of Jesus Christ. We are called to love those who are different from ourselves and particularly those who do not agree with us (Matt. 5:43–44).

Tradition, Tradition

Many years later, in protest, I resigned from association with my Anglican diocese. By this time, national churches from around the world were declaring Canadian Anglicanism to be apostate. However, despite the fact that I had a very deliberate association with dissenting groups of orthodox Anglicans, I couldn't join up with any of them. It wasn't because I couldn't leave the denomination in which I was ordained (although I do love the historical spirituality of that denomination). It was these protesting groups (Bible-centered as they were) who showed no sign of reexamining their old and secure traditions. Few people who were associated with them understood what a Second Reformation might entail. For most of my friends in these groups, realignment and reformation were the same thing.

This reformation required us to reexamine our entire lives; realignment didn't. Those good old days had long lost their effectiveness. But who would risk the leaps required to move into an age of Second Reformation? Verna and I began our search to find a risk-taking church. By this time, we had begun to formulate the questions. But how did we discover them?

In our daily Bible studies, we noticed how we were growing in our appreciation of the style and character of the first-century church. As time went by, we also noticed that we were no longer filtering these insights through the structures and methodology of the Anglican tradition. We had to get out to look in. What we were learning did not compel us to fit those paradigms into our past traditions. It never dawned on us that Jesus' quotation of Isaiah could possibly apply to us. After all, we loved Jesus, and we loved the Bible.

> These people honor me with their lips, but their hearts are far from me. They worship me in vain; their teachings are but rules taught by men. You have let go of the commandments of God and are holding on to the traditions of men. (Mark 7:6–8)

That final addition of Jesus struck us. Could we actually be filtering our kingdom aspirations through Anglicanism? Or were we really filtering absolutely everything through the kingdom of God (Matt. 6:33)? Had the officialdom of the Anglican Church ceased to ask that question?

All too often there is a major difference between thinking through the filters of the denominational church and thinking in the paradigm of kingdom life. What about Lutheranism, Romanism, Methodism, Pentecostalism, etc.? During our journey to other churches, we found that these questions were absolutely valid. But was there ever an age when the church could consistently be credited with putting kingdom priorities first? Not always!

In AD 70, Jerusalem was badly destroyed by the forces of Rome, and it was followed by a massive exile. By the end of the first century, Jerusalem cold no longer be considered the central focus of the whole church. The center of the Roman Empire most certainly gained secular attention. Not surprisingly, the church of Rome, which had gradually taken a major leadership role (because of its place in the Roman Empire) both sought, and was later gradually seen to claim, a unique place of distinction. Before that, the word *catholic* was often used to describe any orthodox Christian. Indeed, by the very late second century, Roman Christians were referring to the first-century church as the Primitive Church.

There were reasons for this, and Professor Paul Stevens of Regent College, Vancouver, refers to one of them. He quotes Hendrick Kramer.

> In the Bible, the laity (Greek, laikoi) is the whole people of God-both clergy and so-called laity ... Christianity arose as an essentially lay movement and it was a long time before "lay" became a term for second-class status ... In addition, with a growing sacramentalism, people demanded that a special person—the priest— dispense the sacraments, while the laity, the "populace," were passive recipients.[2]

With our filters down, Verna and I were able to see that there was absolutely nothing primitive about the church of the first century. Was it structurally one unit? Certainly not! The whole church was far too diverse for that. It was twelve apostles, plus others, like Paul, who were engaged in the work of church planting. Was it one in purpose? In its diversity, yes, it was. Was it one in apostolic belief? Yes, it was, so long as they adhered to the teachings of the twelve apostles. We remember that Peter and others recognized the apostolic authority God had given to Paul (2 Pet. 3:15–17, Gal. 2:9–10). Did they care for one another? Yes, they did. (Read Acts 2 and 4). Did they struggle? Yes! Did they have differences? Yes (Gal. 2:14)! Was it a perfect church? No! But they had one thing that has never been as well emulated in any succeeding century: *They had all the basic principles of the church's purposes in place.* And these principles of belief and practice needed no additions. Succeeding centuries could maintain those principles while adapting them to their own ages. At least they could have, had they looked to the first-century church in its modeling of those essential principles.

---

2   Paul R. Stevens, *Liberating the Laity*. (Downers Grove, IL: InterVarsity Press, 1977), 21.

Questions Emerged

As Verna and I began to examine some first-century principles, questions we could ask of other churches began to form:

1. Structures: Are the structures of this church flexible enough to allow the Spirit to honor essential principles of the first-century church? Do the structures adequately guarantee the authority of apostolic belief? Could those structures embrace those of other churches? For example, the first-century church was never hierarchical in form. Does this church or denomination have the ability to allow the Spirit to challenge present denominational structures at every level?

2. Focus: Is the primary focus of this church inward-looking or outward-looking? For example, does the primary focus enable the desires and wants of the membership, or does it seek God's heart in saving the lost and healing the broken?

3. Worship: Does the worship in this church reflect the form, the informality, and Spirit-led character of the first-century church? Both liturgical and nonliturgical churches may be surprised by our observations.

4. Caring: How well does this church meet the needs of its membership? Interestingly, most churches seemed to score well on this question. Obviously, the first-century church (according to Acts) had a good reputation for this inward focus. The question we often turned to was, "Has this become the primary focus of this church's life?" We will see how the group-based church may provide a healthy perspective on this question (at least as it is applied to first-century principles). Maybe it should go without question, but we did ask ourselves, *"Did we encounter the presence of the Lord in this church?"*

In almost every church Verna and I attended in Calgary, there was an overshadowing pall over them. For many well-meaning people, reformation was fine, but it had to be filtered through the pall and secure filters of their present tradition. Whether we were in a typical Protestant-Evangelical church, or an historical mainline church, in most cases, they all felt that they were following biblical tradition. The problem, in both cases, was that they did not take their tradition back very far. Here, I would also include Roman Catholic, and churches of the Orthodox traditions. *They were not traditional enough!*

There is an ancient letter from Mathetes (which is a Greek word for *disciple*) recorded in the anti-Nicene fathers. It is addressed to a certain Diognetus. Clearly it is the work of an unknown author and written at about the beginning of the second century. It describes Christians to the Roman authorities as follows:

> They dwell in their own countries simply as sojourners. …
> They are in the flesh, but they do not live after the flesh.
> They pass their days on earth, but they are citizens of
> heaven. They obey the prescribed laws, and at the same
> time, they surpass the laws by their lives. They love all
> men but are persecuted by all. They are unknown and
> condemned. They are put to death, but [will be] restored
> to life. They are poor, yet they make many rich. They
> possess few things; yet, they abound in all. They are
> dishonored, but in their very dishonor are glorified. …
> And those who hate them are unable to give any reason
> for their hatred.[3]

A blog on the same subject quotes the following: "At no other time in the history of Christianity did love so characterize the entire church as it did in the first three centuries. And Roman society took note. Tertullian reported that the Romans would exclaim, 'See how they love one another!'"[4] Clearly, in character and purity of purpose, the first-century church deserves to be emulated and given a much closer look.

---

3   Philip Schaff, *Ante-Nicene Fathers, Vol.1,* "Mathetes to Diognetus," chapter 5, Christian Classics Etheral Library (Kindle E Reader).

4   History of the Early Church, "A Love without Condition," www.earlychurch.com/unconditional-love.php, accessed February 13, 2013.

Tradition and Kingdom Priorities

I believe in tradition! What extraordinary character was planted by God into the lives of the believers. And it wasn't at all because they had adopted a different religion. Somehow, in their conversion, the Holy Spirit infused into them the very character of God Himself (Gal. 5:22–26). The believers had eyes that viewed all life through the perspectives of the kingdom of God. With this priority, you may understand why I believe the first-century church (with all its problems and joys) produced all the essential principles that could, and should, be transposed into proceeding centuries.

Being traditional, in the early sense of the word, means that in many ways, the church is counter-culture. But why? It's because the lives, hopes, goals, and values of first-century Christians were set on the kingdom of God. They were not fixed upon a religion or the present and changing culture (Matt. 6:33).

> For here we do not have an enduring city, but we are looking for that city that is to come. (Heb.13:14)

Of course, I'm not speaking of resurrecting first-century life into that of our own. Living in Canada, I don't really relish the idea of huddling over a wood fire every night. However, I sincerely believe the first century does present some very exciting models. *It was actually quite diverse in the way it operated.* The possibilities are very hopeful when we attempt to translate first-century principles into the church of our day.

Clearly the church in Jerusalem wasn't organized in the same way as that in Antioch or Ephesus. I don't think it is possible to find a single form of church organization. Nevertheless, I do think we can identify some common, and essential, principles in the first-century church *that will enable us to translate common principles of apostolic belief and practice into our own age.*

Let's not get sentimental. Not even the first-century church was free of dissension. (It was dissension in Antioch that caused the first general council of the church recorded in Acts 15.) The main problem with the church was and is that there are people in it! It was never a perfect church, but it was still simple, wonderful, and effective. Personally, I have never yet become part of a church community that remained perfect! Nevertheless, I do believe we are called today to struggle with interpreting the principles of what we believe and how we operate as a community.

Present traditions do not escape the sharp-edged penetration of first-century principles. What we believe is called *theology*, and how we organize ourselves to do the work of the church is often called *ecclesiology*. All the principles we need for both are already there in the church of the past. The first-century church utilized the wisdom to allow for a *diversity* of form that clearly honored Jesus Christ as Head and Lord.

I know what you are to read in this book will be really helpful for your church, but there will be lots of reasons your church will probably not go for it. (Later I will mention some of those reasons.) I won't apologize if some were to disagree with me. At my age, it's a waste of time; nobody takes notice of an old coot anyway!

However, there did come a time in my ministry when I wondered whether being a pastor was really worth the pain. But through struggles, I have found out what proves to be my bottom line. When I am real, I know that what matters most is not ego, ambition, or institutional success, *but it's really the kingdom of God that matters, first and foremost* (Matt. 6:33). *That's my bottom line!* It's not always easy to work out, and I'm not good at it, but I know my bottom line is really the kingdom of God, so the most important question is always, *what is best for the kingdom of God?*

The New Testament, in revealing the nature of God (like the journey of Abraham), provides a direction, not a blueprint (Gen.12:1–9). The journey in God and in God's direction produces a way for us to discover contemporary answers to that question.

In my own situation, I had not even discovered most of the fundamentals for working out the question. As far as the institution of the church is concerned, even after eight short years of ordination, there were enough accomplishments to expect to be noticed. (Healing can be slow for some!) But is that what it's all about? My problem was also a good one; I read the Bible an awesome amount. In the New Testament,

I was made aware of a church that admitted to problems, but it was alive!

They were dealing with problems of life, not death. Over and over again, I read of examples of wonderful signs of God's kingdom among His people.

It's All about Relationships

Something happened to those believers in the first century, and it happened from the inside out. They had a personal and intimate relationship with God. Why was that so important? The answer is remarkably simple: *It's because their God revealed Himself to be a relational God.*

We should not be surprised that the four outstanding principles in creation are all linked to relationships. The Bible reveals them to be:

+ relationship with God

+ relationship with God's community

+ relationship with creation

+ relationship with oneself

God Himself exists in a Trinity of persons. I won't try to illustrate what that means by using fancy Greek and Latin words. These are words that attempt to describe the nature of God. But how could manmade words ever accomplish such an impossible feat? After many years, I now realize how extraordinarily wise it was of New Testament writers not to try it. How can manmade words ever describe the awesome and indescribable nature of God? He is and always will be a mystery. Magic can be explained, but mystery never can. (Holy Communion comes into this category.) The apostle Paul also speaks of mystery.

> This grace was given me: to preach to the Gentiles the unsearchable riches of Christ. (Eph. 3:8)

In practical terms, we may see that, if God lives in the perfection of love (because "God is love," 1 John 4:8), then love must have an object. Love must also be capable of *receiving* love. Otherwise, with an eternal, monotheistic God, love would naturally be egocentric. Even before time began, the Trinitarian God would forever go on loving. But who? Himself, of course! The principle of otherness will loom large in this book; it emphasizes an outward focus. I am not speaking of Tritheism, but one God in three Persons. This principle arises from the very nature of our loving Trinitarian God.

Forever and ever, the Father loves the Son who loves the Spirit, who loves the Father, who … Now that's a real circle of love. God is a relational being. It's not surprising that He wants (He doesn't need) a love relationship with His creation. He is therefore the perfection and completion of relationships. God doesn't need our love. (I suspect He could live without mine!) He has decided to extend His love to that which He has made (especially the creation He made in His own image, Gen. 1:26).

If we are called to live our lives in the power of love, then our very purposes for living must be exercised in a stewardship of love. Then there really are some basics of the Christian faith that are essential if we are to take first-century discipleship seriously.

CHAPTER 2

What Are the Basics of Discipleship?

*H*aving sat on many councils of my church denomination, I realize I may have asked questions that caused embarrassment. I may have made assumptions. For example, at every level of the committees concerned with evangelism, we seemed to spend ridiculous amounts of time defining what evangelism is. There was always someone who felt it was presumptuous to invite someone to meet Jesus, especially those who already attended some kind of religious institution, no matter what religion.

Jesus had no problem with the delineation. For the purist in definitions, we realize that Jesus combined both evangelism and mission in a statement encompassing the entire gospel ministry. In His hometown synagogue, He began His ministry of *proclamation and service* by quoting Isaiah. It is easy to separate evangelism and mission, if you want.

> The Spirit of the Lord is on me, because he has anointed me to preach good news to the poor. He has sent me to proclaim freedom for the prisoners and recovery of sight for the blind, to release the oppressed, to proclaim the year of the Lord's favor. (Luke 4:18–19)

That was the entire summary of Christ's ministry! It was written in the Old Testament!

In those committees, the question of when the event of conversion may have occurred was particularly embarrassing. Always there were some people who insisted that it was an indefinable moment. They grew up knowing Jesus. Others would protest that we should not tread on the ground of another person's religion. My response was always quite simple: I'm not concerned about the process of getting there, but can you say, *right now,* that you intimately know Jesus Christ to be your personal Savior and Lord? Sometimes that simple question was answered in anger. I knew the question might be met with resentment. For years I had been bringing people to Christ; many of them had been lifelong churchgoers, like my good friend Glynn.

In the early days of the formation of St. James' Church, Calgary, I told the bishop I wasn't interested in doing church the usual way. It was my ambition to for the decision-makers in the church to have the following qualifications: (1) To be people who were intimately connected with Jesus; (2) to be, obviously, anointed in the power of the Spirit; (3) and to demonstrate that most of their decisions were brought to God in prayer. (I will elaborate on the first two points).

By way of initial preparation, in 1979 I devised a course for that purpose called *Growing in Christ.* It was a seven-session course followed by the laying on of hands and a prayer to accept Jesus into one's life. Glynn was one of the official leaders who attended the seven-session course. Following the last session, on the following Sunday, I asked my usual question: "In two or three minutes, is there anyone who wants to share a thanksgiving to God?"

Immediately Glynn, a highly respected man in his late-fifties, stood up. "Many of you know that I grew up in a preacher's home. I was born on the mission field, and I have occupied most of the leadership roles the church could offer a layman. But I could never say, before last week, what I am about to share with you now. I have just completed our *Growing in Christ* course. For the first time in my entire life, I am able to tell you that *I now know Jesus as my personal Savior and Lord.*"

There was an audible gasp throughout the congregation. This

lifelong church member was admitting to the absence of certain basics of Christian experience. We now had an anointed leader who would pray ceaselessly for guidance of the Holy Spirit. He had certainly been baptized in water, but he admitted that he had appropriated very little of its meaning. Who said church people don't need to appropriate a personal relationship with Jesus? This was to be just the beginning.

In the previous chapter, I was bold enough to suggest that it is possible to hold institutional positions of importance in the Church and yet not realize that basics of Christian experience must first be in place. God showed me the difference. I also began to realize that growth in discipleship must be preceded by certain basics of experience. Now, in sharing my personal basics with you, I am not suggesting that your experience must be the same as mine. Maybe it has come to you slowly. The only question I have is, *"Do you now know that it has come to you?"* (1 John 5:12–13). The basics of essential relationships of which I speak must be personally owned by all of us. The last command Jesus gave to His church was a commission to make disciples. In every one of the gospels, and in the book of Acts, Jesus in some way gave this command:

> All authority in heaven and on earth has been given to me. Therefore go and make disciples of all nations, baptizing them in the name of the Father and of the Son and of the Holy Spirit, and teaching them to obey everything I have commanded you. (Matt. 28:18–20)

We notice that this is a commission containing an imperative verb (in the Greek, *mathaeteusate*). This is a command from the Head of the Church; it is an aorist tense (in a present tense sentence) and reinforces the fact that it is not a suggestion, nor is it debatable. It is complete, and it's a command from the Head of the Church. As such, it has also universal implications (and therefore is intended for people of all religions and in all places). Here, Jesus is saying:

1. He cannot be compared with leaders of any other religion. Jesus is both God and human. Christ's appearing was in the eternal plan of God (1 Pet. 1:19–20).

2. God, being a relational God, desires to have a love relationship with all people He has made. Religion, even Christianity, is not enough; the focus is primarily on a Person, not an institution (John 3:16).

In many of the conferences I was privileged to conduct, clergy or otherwise, I would often ask these questions:

1. How many of you believe in making disciples? Mostly, a rush of hands followed.

2. In your church, how do you actually go about *making* disciples?

I should leave this line blank. The truth is I was all too often met with blank faces.

Strangely, I think it was very soon after my conversion when I began to realize that the process of disciple making began with essential relationships of creation.

There was no point in trying to make disciples of people who could not confess to a personal relationship with Jesus. I found it was the personal relationship with Jesus that turned the focus from an institution to the kingdom of God. Indeed, in that church, the time came when leaders stopped asking the question, "What do I want for my church?" Rather, the question turned to, *"What does Jesus want for His church?"*

Conversion to Jesus

Jesus once said, "I tell you the truth, unless you change and become like little children, you will never enter the kingdom of heaven" (Matt. 18:3). Here, the Greek word used for *change* is *strepo*. In some translations of the Bible, it is written as *convert*. It means the same thing: "to turn and face a new direction." Although I spent my early education in a church school and sang in the church choir, I didn't have a clue what that meant until I was eighteen.

I grew up on the dockland area of Liverpool, England. Once the Beatles got going, everyone knew about the place. Had I been born any closer to the docks, I would have been a dolphin. I was certainly the black sheep of the family, and for some reason, I went to church! It had nothing to do with being religious. In fact, I never let religion get in the way of my real life.

Much of the time I spent my life fighting opposing dock gang members. I was small but busy. (I had a lot more to prove)! But I loved singing, and I loved girls. Church was the best place to get acquainted with both, so I frequented Christ Church, Bootle. The fact is, I can't remember one sermon I ever heard. (They say that subliminal learning has to do for some people.) Maybe I couldn't remember because I spent the sermon time reading racy novels. But when I was about eighteen, some things began to happen. I couldn't explain them with my pea-sized brain.

Possibly I was beginning to wonder if I might end up like some of my gang members. Some of them had been offered two-year holidays (fully paid) by our generous government. None of them seemed able to refuse. These holiday houses were commonly called prisons! One day, a cousin of mine invited me to a religious meeting on a Saturday! What nerve. Who was interested in religion on a Saturday? What an absolute waste of time! Against my natural inclinations, he persuaded me to give up a perfectly good Saturday. So I went.

My first reaction was one of surprise. First of all, they called the event a Youth for Christ rally. It was held in a very large downtown building in Liverpool. That night, Renshaw Hall was crowded, and a lot of the people were my own age. On a Saturday, even! The music was great. It was led by a fantastic pianist who sounded like a sober pub player! The guest speaker, from America, had laryngitis, so his young assistant, a supportive chalk artist, had to fill in. I never did remember what he said or his name, but he drew an artistic impression of a man walking down a winding pathway toward a setting sunset. He asked the enraptured audience, "Where will you be when you reach your sunset?"

I didn't know.

Who thinks of questions like that when you are eighteen? At that age, you have your whole life before you, for goodness sake. Then he did something I had never seen in a church that I had honored with my presence. He asked people to come forward to ask Christ into their lives.

"Why don't you go, Jim?" I asked my cousin.

"I did that a long time ago," he replied.

Nobody went down to the front. The organizers must have felt cheated by the response. I said almost nothing as we travelled back to Bootle on the twenty-eight bus. But I kept on pondering that young guy's question.

Never having been on talking terms with God, I knew I had to say something to Him, so I knelt at the side of my bed and looked at the ceiling. (God is always on the ceiling!) "Lord, I don't know how to talk to you, but I do know my life has to change. Please forgive me for all I've done wrong, and help me to start again."

Nobody had taught me that prayer! I couldn't think of anything else to say, but I remembered that "Amen" was always appropriate. Then I flopped into bed and went to sleep.

At that time, I was an apprentice electrician and working on a very large building site across the River Mersey. In time, the building would become Birkenhead Technical College. For about two weeks, a variety of workmen came up to me and asked the same question: "What's up with you, Alexander? You seem to have changed."

Being in the electrical trade, I was getting used to analyzing puzzling questions, but this one had me stumped. Something *had* changed. For one thing, I had suddenly stopped swearing. Now, I do remember that some months before, I had decided that I should stop my swearing habit. It lasted about fifteen minutes. But I knew it had to be more than attempting to clean up my language. So I said, "I don't know, but whatever it is, it's great!"

Those incidences prompted me to go back to that Youth for Christ thing the very next Saturday. As I walked toward the place, Bill Henderson (whom everyone in Christ Church knew as a "religious nut") approached me. He had a puzzled look on his face.

"Where are *you* going, Charlie?"

I told him, and he nearly passed out. Then he asked me if I had been converted. Converted! I thought the word meant that you changed from being a Protestant to a Catholic.

"Certainly not," I replied.

I didn't know what I was, but I knew what I wasn't.

"Then have you been born again?"

"What's that?" I replied.

As he explained what it was, I felt something bubbling up inside me.

"That's exactly what has happened to me."

As time went by, I began to understand that there were discernible differences of focus in my life. It was the Holy Spirit doing this work all by Himself. Jesus no longer seemed to be a distant figure of history; we were on speaking terms every single day! A natural and daily language that included Jesus was creeping into my normal vocabulary. I used to mention His name every single day before that, but now it was different; it was clean and personal. Jesus said that it would happen.

> But when he, the Spirit of truth comes, he will guide you into all truth … He will bring glory to me by taking from what is mine and making it known to you. (John 16:13–14)

Bill asked me to share my story with a group of young people. They met at Christ Church (Church Army) mission after the Sunday-night service. As I normally attended the "big church," I didn't know many people from the mission. Quite literally, my knees were shaking as I spoke to that young group. After that, I knew one thing for sure; from then on, I would not spend the rest of my life in the electrical business. I would spend it in the power business! And quite remarkably, all of those young people who regularly attended that meeting are still my good friends to this day.

What amazing fellowship! It was truly the beginning of growing in the understanding of what it meant to belong to the body of Christ, to live in the big world of the worldwide church.

However, it was also remarkable that someone like Bill had to tell me I had been born again (John 3:7). It was a perfect description of what God had meant to me in those past few weeks. Obviously, I didn't realize that the Holy Spirit was doing His gentle work of changing me. It took a very long time for me to realize He was beginning to change me into the very image of Jesus Christ (Rom. 8:29). It's a good thing the Holy Spirit doesn't get tired! Also, I soon realized I had not been converted because I decided for Jesus but because Jesus had decided on me.

He has actually decided on everyone, but because we all have free will, not everyone will decide for Him (1 Tim 2:4). My yes to Jesus was simply my response to His gracious calling upon my life.

At the time, I didn't realize this conversion thing is something that goes on and on and on. After many years, I began to understand that what had happened to me had absolutely nothing to do with religion.

The basic truth of the matter was that I never did get converted to Christianity. I was converted to a person—Jesus Christ. I really wasn't converted to a religion or an institution, such as Christianity or Buddhism or something else. That would have meant I had to understand the nature of the religion and begin its religious search with all its philosophy, rules, and disciplines, etc. It wasn't even Christianity that accounted for the dramatic change in my life. I couldn't compare it with any another religion. It was a personal relationship with God, and the Holy Spirit insisted on pointing me to a very close and personal relationship with Jesus.

The Christian way is simply this: *If you want to know God, you do it through Jesus (Matt. 11:27, John 14:9). The other way around doesn't work.* After all, the man Christ Jesus is also God! From then on, I wasn't calling people to Christianity but to the person of Jesus Christ. Just last week, a young man asked me the question, "What is truth?" He may not have known that Pilate, the Roman governor, asked Jesus the same question (John 18:38). Maybe he thought we should enter into some kind of philosophical debate. He was surprised by my answer: "Truth is not about philosophy; it's about a person, Jesus Christ. The Christian faith is all about relationships, beginning with Him."

When I think of it now, the fact is, I wouldn't die for a religion—any religion. But I hope I would have the courage to die for Jesus.

For many years after that, God privileged me to lead hundreds and thousands of people to a personal relationship with Jesus, and many of those people were solid churchgoers! Had it not been for that awareness, my formal theological training would have killed me. It would have just been a subject, a religiously academic subject. Often I felt very sorry for students who had lovely and noble intentions but felt they had been "called to the church." This fundamental principle has guided all my thinking throughout my Christian life. It's not just my opinion; it's very biblical. It is also common experience in the entire historical tradition of the church.

The process of conversion may be very slow or very fast. The length of time, or how it happens, is not the issue at all. The point is, do you know Jesus personally as your Savior right now? Biblically and personally speaking, I am not surprised that the first plank on the pathway of discipleship is entering into a personal relationship with Jesus. But that brings us to *something more of the Spirit's work in us*. There is always something more, because no one has ever arrived.

The Holy Spirit and Supernatural Power

Astoundingly, after three years of apprenticeship with the Master, Christ's disciples heard this from Him:

> I am going to send you what my Father has promised;
> but stay in the city until you have been clothed with
> power from on high." (Luke 24:49)

This request was another reversal of what a guru of religion would say to his disciples. The religious teacher would somehow tell his pupils that they had graduated and were now capable of going out to teach others. Jesus told His disciples to stay where they were (in Jerusalem) until something would happen to them. They would get power. It would be a Word plus power ministry. But power for what? Jesus said this:

> I tell you the truth, anyone who has faith in me will do
> what I have been doing. He will do even greater things
> than these, because I am going to the Father. (John
> 14:12)

Here Jesus told His disciples that their future work would not be simply teaching. They had to do what they were teaching. They weren't giving history lessons. Their future ministry would, in reality, be in doing the things Jesus did. Their work, like His, would demonstrate (i.e., would be signs) of what the kingdom of God was all about. "Don't just talk about it, do it! There are twelve of you, there was just one of me. Between you, there will be greater things. You have had enough teaching, but *you haven't got the power to do what I'm asking of you.*" That's my own paraphrase, but it will do!

After spending all of those years in college, I was never asked whether I had experienced this power. Should not that have been a condition for graduation? Oh, yes, I really did love Jesus. And oh yes, I had led many, many people to Him. But did I really know what it meant to be a disciple-maker? Somewhere, sometime, I had to wait in my Jerusalem. I had to wait for my Pentecost. As a future leader, somewhere, sometime, I should have been led to wait in my Jerusalem.

Led by God, Reluctantly

I find it difficult to claim the Holy Spirit didn't operate in my life until after a baptism in the Spirit experience. After all, how could I have been brought to a living relationship with Jesus without the work of the Holy Spirit (John 16:13)? I am not saying a person can't experience the Spirit's leading apart from some further experience. (Actually, life in the Spirit entails *a lot of empowering experiences.* After Pentecost, note a further empowering in Acts 4:31.) At one time, my pastor in Christ Church, Bootle, said I should go to the Prairies of Canada to study for ordination.

He went there. I didn't want to go. I didn't have to. Canada? Who would go there, willingly? I had already gone through the hoops in England and had been accepted as a postulant for ordination. Besides, for about seven years, I had a relationship with Rita, a girl from Christ Church. It was an on-off relationship. It was on with me but off with her! Why should I leave my beloved England to go and preach in a wheat field in Saskatchewan? And then there was the matter of Rita. She would never follow me to Canada.

In order to stop my vicar nagging at me, I had gone to London to ask the staff of the Colonial and Continental Church Society (now the Commonwealth and Continental Church Society) why I should go to Canada. I wasn't impressed, so I came back home and forgot all about it. However, one day Ina Weaver, a lady in church, spoke to me. She was the wife of the local Church Army captain from Christ Church Mission.

"Charlie, I have been thinking about you all week, and the Lord gave me a verse of Scripture for you."

With an abundance of bored disinterest, I asked her what the verse was.

"Get out of your country to a land that I will show you" (Gen. 12:1). Then she asked me, "What does it mean?"

I nearly shouted her head off. "Nothing!" I retorted loudly.

With one verse of Scripture, no one was going to mess up my life. I tried to forget it, but in those days, when an Anglican quoted Scripture, people tended to think something was wrong. I thought that at least I should pray about it. Now I'm not one of those people who do the Gideon thing when I want an answer from God. In that process, we tell God how He is going to reveal His will! That fleece event happened on one occasion to Gideon (Judges 6:36–40), so I thought I would give it one shot. I have never done it since. Putting God at the end of our own criteria for guidance is usually not the way of the Spirit.

"Lord, if I ever see a boat ticket in my hand for Canada, I'll go."

I felt really safe because there was no way I would ever buy a boat ticket to go to such a *foreign country*. I had a great sleep that night. About two weeks later, I opened up a letter, and the first thing to fall out was a boat ticket to Canada. It was that society in London. They took my interest to be an application. Maybe God had presumed that I meant it when I said I would go, if …! But I had put my conditions for His consideration. I didn't know He could be so personal. About six weeks later, on August 16, 1961, I was aboard the Cunard ship *Saxonia*. I was destined for Canada. During that week of sailing, I left more fluid on the ship than was under it.

For the entire first term at Emmanuel College, Saskatoon, I insisted on telling God how much He owed me. He didn't argue. I reminded God of His Word and told Him He wasn't so good at keeping it.

> Delight yourself in the Lord and he will give you the desires of your heart. Commit your way to the Lord; trust in him, and he will do this. (Ps. 37:4–5)

Soon, after Christmas, Rita wrote me a letter. She told me that she had gotten herself engaged, and to a really good friend of mine. I was absolutely shattered!

"God, You owe me! God, Your Word isn't true."

I was referring to the above verse of Scripture. In fact, I reminded Him of it every day after leaving England.

After a few months of wrestling with God, I abandoned everything to Him. "I won't question You anymore on this, Lord. I'll stay where You want me to be."

At the end of my first year, the bishop of Brandon asked me if I would spend the summer at a place called Russell in Manitoba. The pastor had experienced a heart attack, so they needed someone there quickly. They had never had a student minister there before. Most certainly, they have never had one since! On the first Sunday, after the morning service, Lillian Glasman introduced me to her daughter. It took me all of two weeks to realize I had met the "desire of my heart." After forty-seven years of marriage, Verna remains the delightful joy of my heart. I think I'll keep dating her. As the enthusiastic African Christians say, "The Lord is good. All the time, the Lord is good." I became slightly inclined to believe His word is true!

In spite of all I have said, I believe it to be of great importance for all Christians continually to seek after the enabling of the Holy Spirit. We can't move very far simply with just our own natural gifts, but many try. I didn't know it, but that's precisely what I was doing.

After six years of ordination and ministering in Manitoba, I was invited by my former college principal to share ministry with him in Calgary. They were three wonderful years. But I was becoming dissatisfied. It wasn't about a change in location, but the Bible was bothering me.

Now I Know Something about Pentecost

Every time I read the book of Acts, I saw believers whose lives were vibrant testimonials to the power of the gospel. Clearly, the Holy Spirit was enabling them with supernatural gifts of healings, miracles, etc. Why wasn't it happening in my ministry? Jesus said it would, and it didn't. I didn't know why I was unhappy with my ministry, but later I defined it as a divine dissatisfaction. What on earth is that? The Holy Spirit was creating a hunger in me to come closer to Him. He taught me that I was operating on the basis of my own ego, my own ambition, my own natural talents, and the naïve belief that I could find the answers to all of the questions arising in my ministry.

Those early Christians were living in an awesome state of anticipation. They believed God was able to perform, through His people, all the things He had ordered. Signs and wonders were plentiful. The result was that the church just kept on growing (Acts 5:12–16)! I couldn't think of many places anywhere in North America where all that biblical stuff was happening on a regular basis. Yet I knew that was the way it was supposed to be. Isn't that why the bishop laid hands on me at my ordination? I was in for a surprise! It was to be another thing I couldn't explain. *Incidentally, I define a charismatic person as one who is able to be surprised by God!*

In 1973, I was invited to conduct a clergy retreat in Brandon. My old pal Bob Reed was there. We had worked close together in Northern Manitoba. Close? Verna and I were in Snow Lake while Bob and Barbara were in Lynn Lake, a short distance of about two hundred miles through the bush. Now that he was ministering in Brandon, Bob invited me back to his house. He and Barbara began to share what God was doing in their ministry.

"Bob, you have been converted," I countered. That was all the language I knew, so that's what it must have been.

"I was converted years ago," Bob replied. "The difference in both of our lives now is the power of the Holy Spirit."

As I was quickly letting myself out of the front door, I countered, "I am going to pray for you, Bob."

"And I'm sure going to pray for you," was the loud reply.

I think he won!

That night I was in Neepawa, the place where, for four years, we were in ministry before we came to Calgary. I was staying at the house of my good friends, Ed and Marie Salway. That night, while lying in bed, I found myself reading John 15. For the first time, the fifth verse really got to me.

Apart from me you can do nothing. (John 15:5)

"Nothing, nothing?" I was really mad at God. After all the hard work I had done for Him, He was telling me I could do nothing without Him. I was so angry I threw my Bible against the wall.

Coming from Liverpool, and having an Irish temper, Liverpool people usually and quite quickly forget why they are mad. As my temper settled down, suddenly I felt a peace that seemed to possess my entire being. I had a great sleep. When I arrived back in Calgary, of course, I told Verna about it. I didn't know what had happened. However, within two days, I had prayed for a man with a long-standing heart problem. In the intensive care unit *I found myself thanking God for His healing.* Thanking God for His healing? The doctor had just informed the family, in my presence, that Bill would not last the night. Bill was healed, and the following morning a surprised staff nurse informed me that Bill was sitting up and eating his breakfast! Three months later, Bill was doing tasks he hadn't been able to do for five years.

There was one thing I knew for sure: *I didn't do it!* That's when I began to understand how the apostle Peter felt when he commanded the lame man to walk (Acts 3:1–10). Professionals of the religious establishment were mad at him because Peter mentioned that Jesus had done the healing! The Holy and Righteous One, the Author of life, had done this miracle on a Sabbath! This miracle worker was the one whom God had raised from the dead. Peter was like a little boy who was caught with his hand in the cookie jar. "I didn't do it. Jesus did it! Jesus did it!"

As for me, I was beginning to realize what was happening: *It was a breakthrough of the Holy Spirit in offering the something more of what is always possible from God.*

Once again, something of great significance had happened to me, and I couldn't explain it. Like my conversion to Jesus, something of a supernatural nature had occurred. Mr. Fixit didn't have the answers! Now I have many more questions.

There was a strange pastor in Calgary who kept on talking that way. Most clergy would often walk on the other side with a white stick when they saw him coming. I swallowed my pride and arranged to see him. When I told Fred Dykes what was happening, he just laughed and said, "Now you know for yourself. You have been baptized in the Holy Spirit."

Clearly, we have the assurance right now that, with a repentant heart, and aware of our own inadequacies, we can receive the anointing of the Spirit for the work to which He called us. In my own experience, I have learned one important thing: *It's not so much a question of how much I possess of the Holy Spirit but how much the Holy Spirit possesses of me.*

The vast majority of my questions are not about the frequency of supernatural events but the infrequency of them, especially in the Western world.

It's much too important for us to be debating theology here. However it happens, and however long it takes, it is vitally important to know that we can operate in Holy Spirit power now! Verna had been longing for something more of the Holy Spirit for a long time. All she received from me were trite theological answers. On the next Sunday evening, we decided to attend St. Luke's evening service. Fred laid hands on Verna, and immediately she broke out in tongues. A few days earlier, in the quietness of our living room (no one was around), I also broke out in tongues. It sounded Chinese to me. I wondered if my mother had forgotten to tell me something. Every day, from that time on, Verna and I have prayed to God in this beautiful gift of tongues. It seems to be a vehicle to release other gifts of the Spirit. If you know Jesus yet wonder why charismatic gifts appear as a rarity in your life, maybe it would be a good idea to meet with a person who is regularly accustomed to the administration of these gifts. Possibly, you may need what the apostle Paul calls an *impartation* (Rom. 1:11, Acts 19:6).

All of this was not a one-shot event. Not long after, I was conducting a conference in a place called Rimbey in central Alberta. The family I was staying with was very upset. Their married daughter had been diagnosed with cancer of the uterus. That next week, she was due for surgery. During the week, she came to the night sessions. I told her we would be glad to pray for her, but she did not respond to the invitation. However, on the Friday evening, she did receive prayer for healing.

The very next Tuesday she was in the hospital in Red Deer. The operation went on as planned. However, not long after the surgery, the surgeon visited Ruth. He looked embarrassed.

"What is wrong?" Ruth inquired.

"I don't know how to apologize," the surgeon replied. "We took out the uterus, as planned, but all subsequent tests affirm there is no cancer in the tissue."

Ruth, who already had three children, laughed. "It's all right. Don't be concerned. God has healed me."

About two years later, I received a phone call from her. She was doing well. "It's about Dad. He has cancer, but we are going to bring him to Calgary to get healed."

I was ready to offer excuses, but Ruth wouldn't hear of it. "God healed me. Now, he is going to heal my dad."

I was reminded of the faith of those four people who let a paralyzed friend down through a roof. Jesus healed the man on the basis of their faith (Mark 2:3–12). A few days later, David Brown (her former pastor) and I had a little communion service at St. James' Church. During the service, we both laid hands on Dad. He was completely healed! His doctor later confirmed it.

The previous examples are just a small illustration of the importance of beginning a discipleship process with people who know Jesus and who desire to operate in the supernatural power of the Spirit.

Indeed, I would go so far as to say that there is little point in starting anything of significance in a congregation until a substantial portion of the congregation knows Jesus in personal terms and is already experiencing the power of the Holy Spirit through signs and wonders. Obviously, the preparation process is of the utmost importance.

Everything is really all about the character of the kingdom of God, particularly as we see it demonstrated in Eden. The Eden community was given power to do God's commission (Gen. 1:28). In other words, they were inbreathed to make what was supernaturally possible concerning what God intended at the beginning (Gen. 2:7). Many people in various churches may want to move in this direction. The questions are: Does my church consider itself to be ready to move in this direction? And once in process, how do ordinary people get to do Spirit-empowered ministry?

CHAPTER 3

Do You Have a Process for Making Disciples?

A Method in Our Madness

There's a lot of wisdom in following principles borne in prayer. If we don't know where to start, then we don't know where we are headed. We shouldn't determine the end of a process because what God wants for our churches is entirely up to Him. But He does work hard to give us the first pieces of the puzzle. After several years of ordination, I realized that the process of discipleship, on which I had embarked, might easily be summed up in the following acrostic: METRE.

Here is how it looks as we applied it at St. James' Church:

M-Motivation

At the heart of all we are and do is the foundation of our relationships. Why is that? *It's because our God, who is one in a Trinity of Persons, is a relational God.* The primary thing we do as a Christian community is to demonstrate our life in relation to God, to others, and to His creation. And as we have seen, the order doesn't begin with ourselves (as we are often told in this me-centered world). So where do we start in our churches?

In 2009, with my good friend, John Briscall, Bishop Terry Buckle invited us to speak at a clergy conference in Whitehorse in the Yukon. On one occasion, I mentioned the seven-session course that, by God's grace, I had devised for St. James' Church. It was entitled *Growing in Christ*. Little did I know that an Anglican church in Bromley, England, had a similar idea! The program that emerged was called *Alpha*. It has proven to be enormously anointed, and has been used very effectively throughout the world. However, Alpha was designed for *those who are not already in church*. I was looking for something that related to those *who were already regularly attending church*. And so, *Growing in Christ* appeared by divine inspiration! It has been used widely, and sometimes churches use it after Alpha.

"I began teaching *Growing in Christ* in 1980," (At that time Hope Lutheran church graciously accommodated us; that is until we grew too big).

"No, it wasn't," a lady responded from the back of the hall. "It was in 1979. The first one took place in your living room, and I was there. It was a powerful influence on me and my future ministry."

To my surprise, I recognized her but didn't know she had been ordained. This was the same session Glynn had attended. For further information on this course, and others, please see the web page: www.timothyministry.ca.

In that quickly growing congregation, we were able to put on that event twice a year for many years. (Eventually it was presented by Sheila van de Putten, a so-called layperson who was gifted in teaching.) Another course, *Growing in Discipleship*, followed after. But the purpose of GIC had a threefold edge:

1. To bring people to a personal and living relationship with God.

2. To experience the supernatural life of the Spirit in making real the power to do ministry.

3. To work out the reality of commitment to Christ. Conversion to Christ means conversion to the Body of Christ.

Those three factors proved to be the right motivation. For one thing, people were beginning to lose their churchy baggage. Their language changed from the institutional language of the church to the very personal language of *Jesus*. We heard far more people ask the question, "What is good for the kingdom of God?" "What is good for our church?" seemed to be lost in the mists of iniquity. They were excited about bringing people to Christ. Bringing people to church was a secondary issue. The quality of prayer changed considerably. (I would say that the quality of personal prayer life proved to be a third of the discipleship basics that were developing.)

Of course, like most churches, we lived with lots of problems. But like many other churches, and as the years rolled by, prayer was at the heart of everything we did. This was especially true for those in decision-making positions. In time, we were able to set criteria for anyone taking roles of leadership: *First,* they had to have participated in a *Growing in Christ* course, and *second,* they had to be people who naturally made prayer part of their daily and decision-making life. For example, in our council meetings, there were often times when we spent more time in prayer than in discussion.

We felt much joy as people travelled long distances to be part of our community. One family regularly drove fifty-odd miles from the mountainous Kananaskis country to participate in what God was doing in our community. We had begun ministry at St. James' by building foundations on substance and not on sand or even on anachronistic traditions. We felt God urged us not to be trapped by traditions that are no longer effectively supportive of gospel motivation (Mark 7:6–7). Indeed, Jesus really did encourage the *renewal of gospel systems* that focused on what was best for the kingdom rather than what is in keeping with the manmade historic traditions of the institution.

> And no one puts *new wine* into old wineskins. If he does, the wine will burst the skins, and both the wine and the wineskins will be ruined. No, he pours new

wine into *new wineskins*. (Mark 2:22, italics mine. The
Greek of *new wine—neon onion*—speaks of wine newly
made. Its effervescent and lively activity would burst old
wineskins, but *fresh wineskins* are described as *askous
kainous*. The plural case speaks of wineskins that have
been beaten out and stretched to accommodate the life
of new wine—structures that undergo renewal.)

In other words, we will look at the value of diversity but also note
that old and inflexible wineskins should never be allowed to hinder the
moving and vibrant life of the Spirit. *Those wineskins will not support and
accommodate Spirit life, which often disturbs what is for it to become what
God desires.*

At St. James, we were learning to let God stretch the old wineskins.
No wonder this growing church was considered to be very odd by many
of the established and institutional mind-set. We were joining with
many renewal-minded churches that possessed a *meta-mind-set*. In
other words, we were open to Spirit-inspired *change*. Understanding
the sloppiness that can follow the mindless desire for change, we soon
came to this conclusion: The church must move into new times and
changing cultures under the principle that *the gospel never changes, but
its methodology must.*

Don Posterski, a Christian sociologist, notes,

Effective churches are those which build on the strengths
of four cornerstones: orthodoxy-in touch with truth;
community-in touch with personal needs; relevance-in
touch with the times; outreach-in touch with the needs
of others.[5]

But maybe, like me, you wonder if those four points really capture all

5   Don Posterski, *Where's a Good Church?* (Winfield, British Columbia: Wood
Lake Books, 1993), 19.

the power of a first-century church that looks constantly to the surprises of signs and wonders of the Spirit.

E-Education

> Always be prepared to give an answer to everyone who asks you to give the reason for the hope that you have. (1 Pet. 3:15)

God is not honored by ignorance. We are expected to know what we are talking about. The apostle Paul once said, "I know whom I have believed, and am convinced that he is able to guard what I have entrusted to him for that day" (2 Tim. 1:12). In other words, *personal experience must be supported by historic revelation.*

The writer to Jude agrees.

> I ... urge you to contend for the faith that was one for all entrusted to the saints. (Jude 3)

Subjective experience is not good enough, if it is not tested by the above historic criteria. Even in the early days of the 1980s, we were in a pluralistic generation that usually spoke in existential and relative terms: "That is very nice for you, but my experience is different."

By simply comparing subjective experiences, we were supposed to abandon absolute truth in favor of *individual spirituality.* Of course, that attitude has been firmly cemented in the twenty-first century. All such attitudes well suit a globalized economy but not globalized truth. The point was, we were worshipping in a building in a reasonable proximity to the University of Calgary. A good number of the various faculty staff, and a strong sprinkling of students, attended the church. Many members agreed that we needed to have a substantive reason concerning why we were Christians in search of the truth and not just people seeking a spirituality suiting their own personal needs.

When We Began Home Groups

Robin Guinness and the congregation of St. Stephen, Montreal, were doing some interesting things. What appealed to us was the fact that this Montreal church placed a heavy emphasis on home groups. Having previously conducted a conference at that church, I felt free to ask Robin to hop over the nearly three thousand miles. And so, on invitation, Robin kindly travelled all the way to Calgary. He spent a day with a large group of eager learners. Thanks to Robin, the home-group principle appealed to us as being a strong biblical principle. Even today, it is still a very important part of the life of St. James' Church.

Nevertheless, it would take quite a number of years for me to learn that *there is a significant difference between a group-based church and a program church that includes home groups.* (At that time, group-based churches were hard to find. I hadn't even heard of one!) As we will see, the group-based church is pivotal and foundational to the entire structure of the ministering congregation. In mainline churches, this reality easily becomes a bit troubling because, naturally, it crosses with expectations and structures of many historic denominations. At some point, the group-based church will certainly lock horns with historic, orthodox churches.

To get to where we were, we did learn that, to help people prioritize how they used their time, we decided to hold the *home group twice a month, not every week.* On the weeks between, we held our teaching sessions on what we called, "Tuesday Night at St. James." It was very popular. Sometimes there would be four or five sessions going on at the same time. Newcomers were expected to do a *Growing in Christ* course, while others may have engaged themselves in biblical studies, *Growing in Discipleship,* pastoral ministry courses, social conditions and needs in the local area, using spiritual gifts, etc. The clergy did not determine the education needs, although they did have input. Group leaders met together and relayed education needs as the groups identified their needs. (We even accommodated a Greek course!)

Of course, no one is gifted to enable and teach all of those various sessions. We must kill off the absurd notion that the ordained pastor is *able.* Obviously, we asked for help from social workers, police, doctors, and pastors known for their special gifting (and they came from a variety of denominations). We got the very best people we could, and we were generous in our giving of honorariums. We operated always on the principle: *If we order the agenda, we pay the bills. If God sets the agenda, He provides the resources.*

And it worked time and time again. God was generous to us, so we were generous to others. Soon we had a full-time clerical staff of three, plus a youth worker and secretarial and cleaning persons. God ordered it. No one ever went short on salary. At that time, my two dear friends Mike and Phil were in affirmed leadership positions. Largely, it was they who kept me remembering that our budget was never the criteria for doing ministry. Because the leadership prayed hard concerning God's agenda for ministry the next year, we actually gave away our surplus at the end of every year. And there was always a surplus. God doesn't seem to be able to count as well as our church accountants! Whatever God had ordered, He would make the resources available. They were scary days! Tuesday Night at St. James' proved to be a very exciting and enabling occasion. It was good to be in an environment where people were becoming well qualified in what they were doing.

T-Training

Of course, training, education, and practice go hand in hand. Nevertheless, in the area of charismatic gifts, there had to be a great deal of spiritual wisdom involved and also wise guidance on how those gifts were to be used. That is not to put restraints on what the Holy Spirit can do. Experience taught me that the *charismatic life* could be enabled through people who would not be limited by their natural abilities.

We made spiritual gifts inventories available to everyone, but that was to enable the community to recognize how, in general terms, the Holy Spirit normally worked in individual lives. *However, we should be available to God anytime, anyhow, and anywhere.* I believe an ongoing, practical training process would be normal in a properly focused home group church. We'll get to that later.

Spiritual gifts are not confined to charismatic gifting. Natural gifts are also spiritual when they are offered to the glory of God and the honoring of His kingdom. Let's have a look at most of them, particularly as they appear in the New Testament:

Spiritual Gifting
(Rom. 12:4–8; 1 Cor. 12:4–11; Eph. 4:11)

Charismatic	Natural
Prophecy	Personal Skills
Wisdom	Wisdom
Knowledge	Knowledge
Faith	Cheerfulness
Healing	Giving
Miracles	Compassion
Discernment	Leadership
Tongues	Hospitality
Interpretation	Craftsmanship
of Tongues	

What about humor? The apostle Paul didn't seem to display it as a spiritual gift. I'm sure that, in my ministry, God gets a good laugh, so He has a sense of humor! Did you notice that wisdom and knowledge are found in both categories?

We should note that natural gifts often manifest themselves in ministries of justice. In the book of Isaiah, the word *justice* is mentioned as being intrinsically connected to the very nature of God: "For I the Lord love justice …" (Isa. 61:8). However, even in church deliberations of today, the word is sometimes abused and sentimentalized to secure personal agendas. What is justice to one becomes oppression to others. So what is justice?

By my count, in the book of Isaiah alone on ten occasions the word *justice* is accompanied by the word *righteousness*. In other words, God's revealed righteousness is the yardstick by which *justice is understood*. It must be consistent with the revealed nature of God. But to get back to our broader view of spiritual gifting, in these days of rapidly diminishing congregations in the West, we hear of fast growth in places like Africa and the southern globe.

Once when I was attending a conference in England, I asked an

African participant why the African church was growing so rapidly. Without hesitation, and with a big smile on his face, he replied, "Because of signs and wonders." The conversation moved to methods of discipleship. Suddenly his face took on a much more serious appearance. In a somber voice, he retorted, "Our problem is not one of bringing people to Christ and to an anointing of the Spirit; it is one where such people are often poorly trained and thrust into the leadership of several congregations. Consequently, we have situations in which people are playing at a spirituality that embraces both Jesus Christ and animism."

I want to suggest that problems in the Western church are very similar today. We also have severe problems of mediocre leadership. Even though the reasons may not be identical, nevertheless, all too often we hear of leadership that takes its values from the culture and the media while professing allegiance to Jesus. Gabe Lyons expresses the same concern in this way:

> I believe this moment is unlike any other time in history. Its uniqueness demands an original response. If we fail to offer a different way forward, we risk losing entire generations to apathy and cynicism. Our friends will continue to drift away, meeting their need for spiritual transcendence through other forms of worship and communities of faith that may be less true but more authentic and appealing.[6]

Tuesday Night at St. James' may not have reached Everest standards of training, but it was an attempt, in process, to match training with spiritual gifting.

R-Releasing

"That was a great sermon on the ministry of laypeople," Mike told me. Before the other shoe dropped (Mike had shown he was good at offering affirmation, but …) I waited for it. "The problem is I don't think you can do it." Clang!

---

6   Gabe Lyons, *The Next Christians*. (New York: Doubleday Religion, 2010), 11.

Around Mike, there was no point in wearing both shoes! One would fall off anyway! He sat me down in my office while he towered over me. At five foot five (and a half), I thought I should practice being a good listener!

Mike proceeded to tell me what most clergy really know. Sometimes they are reluctant to put it into practice. Jesus put it into practice when He sent out the twelve. After that, He also sent out the seventy. In his working life, Mike was in an executive position in a worldwide oil company.

"You are still holding on to power. The ministry of this church doesn't belong to you; it belongs to all the God-anointed people."

"Well, I know that!"

"Well, why don't you get out of the way and let them get on with it?"

I didn't know what he meant.

"You have done a great job in teaching and training the people, but they still look to you for permission to set in motion their gifting."

It began to dawn on me that, without me, the leadership was not yet free to *initiate*, to *organize*, to *fail*, or to *succeed*. They were doing jobs for me while I was telling them they were doing jobs for God. If someone was responsible for the outreach of the church, then the entire ministry was theirs, not mine. Unfortunately, in many churches, so-called laypeople think the ministry in which they are gifted belongs to the pastor. And pastors believe it when they boast of how much they delegate ministry to the laypeople. If they delegate, then the ministry still belongs to the clergy. In my own denomination, that order is usually accepted without question. Things began to change!

Sometime later, after a Sunday service, there was a knock on my office door.

"Charles, I want you to know that I won't be able to teach the baptism class next Sunday."

I had spent a couple of months training about five people to do what was always assumed of the clergy. We had two other full-time clergy around, but those five so-called laypeople had become well equipped and had scored strongly on their spiritual gifts inventory. The lady who knocked on my door was a professional teacher and worthy of running that entire ministry. She was the leader.

"Why are you telling me?" I asked her.

"I thought that you ought to know," she replied.

"A couple of months ago, didn't we bring the five of you before the congregation, and didn't we lay hands on you, and didn't we appoint you to be the leader?"

"Yes."

"Then I don't want to know," I said, in termination of the conversation.

"Oh, is that what you really mean when you call me the leader?"

"It's all yours," I replied.

She went away very happy. On my part, I knew that it was the beginning of a ministry where Jesus was the Head, *and I was responsible to enable, encourage, and release what God had gifted in others.*

Spending Too Much Time in Church

In all too many churches, there is an unspoken assumption that the more time we spend at church, the more we are growing in discipleship. A lot of church people need to get a life! Most people live with a lot of diverse interests today: family, work, community interests, sports, recreational interests, TV, taxiing children, etc. They are all good grounds for having fun and witnessing for the gospel of Jesus.

I remember that at St. James, Calgary, one middle-aged mother of teenagers consistently volunteered for numerous jobs that needed doing in the church. She seemed to spend more time in the church than at home! Eventually her husband stopped coming altogether. One day, she came to see me with a sad burden on her heart.

"I pray every day for him to come back, but he will have nothing to do with the church anymore."

"It's not surprising," I said.

She was perplexed.

"I am asking you to drop everything you are doing in this church! Spend your time with your husband and family."

Tearfully, she agreed. Consequently, in a few months, her husband was back and proudly holding the hand of his long-lost wife. In time, this, and what we were learning, helped us to draw up some basic expectations for serious membership:

Expectations in Ministry

1. Commitment to God,
2. Commitment to prayer
3. Commitment to my family life,
4. Commitment to the worshipping life of the congregation,
5. Commitment to one area of growth and nurture.
6. Commitment to one area of ministry.

In the process of taking seriously what it means to be one of a priesthood of all believers (1 Pet. 2:9), heads of commissions were appointed—not heads of committees. The committees were the major visionaries and supporters for commissions to which they belonged. We couldn't call the leaders elders, but they really were. It wasn't very Anglican! But do you know something? *The same problem exists in all the denominations of the Christian church. Pastors must surrender control to those the Spirit has gifted for ministry.* (There is a major difference between control and enabling leadership.)

The late David Watson of York, England, in his book, *Discipleship*, often lamented that clergy became the cork in the bottle. Usually they stifle the life of the Spirit. This is especially true when the Spirit starts movement from the bottom upward. Does this mean pastors have no authority anymore? No, it doesn't. But we'll get to that later when we discuss the nature and purpose of home groups.

Meanwhile, back at St. James, elders began to take upon themselves real ownership, responsibility, and encouragement. Also, they were accepting accountability and encouragement for the ministries in which they have been gifted, affirmed, and trained.

This was the end of me as pastor standing up in church asking for *volunteers.* For one thing, we adopted a principle that, apart from elders of commissions, *people should not be asked to remain in a particular position for more than three years.* Second, replacements were raised up from within the ministry commission itself. *All ministries were self-duplicating.* The result was that there were no more appeals for volunteers.

On some occasions, volunteers may be necessary, but usually just for jobs anyone may do at that time. The work of an elder for ministry, such as evangelism or feeding the poor, is to raise leadership from within his or her portfolio. The local church council would affirm and give authority to a new elder while the leading elder would be affirmed and ordained at the level of the wider church but in consultation with the local congregation.

Of course, initiative for new ministries usually arose from the commissions themselves. One of those initiatives helped me to appreciate how Jesus felt. "I watched Satan fall from heaven like a flash of lightning" (Luke 10:18). Having sent out the seventy, they reported back. Similarly, the missions commission, through prayer, felt a call to witness in other places and churches.

They organized a couple of teams, and called the events "People-to-People Missions." With a little training with the leaders, we laid hands on all involved and sent them out. The number of places asking for these lay-led missions really amazed us at St. James. But the greater joy was their sharing of the wonderful things God had done through them. We all grew as a result of this outward focus on ministry.

E-Evaluation

Suppose that, if I owned a business, and if I had to look after the books, both I and the employees would soon be lining the walls of an employment agency. On my part, in church ministry, and never knowing what people gave or handling money, meant that the church would be in great shape, especially if gifted people were to come together in a networking manner. Actually, I had learned from businesspeople in the congregation that their companies periodically set aside a time to ask questions, such as: "Have we met our goals? Did we make any money? What went wrong? What did we do well? How may we improve?"

What if a newcomer to the church asked you the questions: "How do you go about implementing your mission statement? How is it going?" What would be your answer?

It has been my practice to call the entire congregation together for a Saturday about every two years, at the least. The purpose has been to look at basic questions concerning the work of the kingdom of God in our area. I realized that, without evaluation being part of the process, frustration often set in, people became angry and impatient, and some just threw in the towel. (With an apostolic focus, the twelve apostles, after Pentecost, certainly sought guidance from the Holy Spirit. They wanted to know His plan for their universal mission). These were the kind of questions we would ask in that day session:

Evaluating Ministry

1. How effective have we been in pursuing goals of the past?

2. What did we do well?

3. What did we not do well? How may we do better?

4. What are our priorities today?

5. Who has the gifts for this ministry?

6. How should it be done?

7. Does the present structure of church life best facilitate these goals?

8. How are we trained, empowered, and released?

Often our questions were far too penetrating. They exposed weaknesses in the overall structure of our denomination. At times, those structures put limitations upon us. Of course, we also realized that this business of evaluation isn't a thing that's done only once. It goes on and on. Before further evaluation, a church cannot know where it is going and how, unless the ministries are given about two years to discover their strengths and weaknesses.

CHAPTER 4

Obedience Brings Surprises

*A*t St. James Church, we were growing in our understanding of using spiritual gifting. To use one ministry as an example, all the clergy were accountable for their pastoral work to a dentist. In one role of leadership, Phil Greeves had become the affirmed head of all pastoral ministries. He was a great encourager, and about twice a month, he left his dental practice for a whole morning to meet with the clergy. He was also a great listener who had a pastoral heart. He regularly brought all pastoral ministries together for prayer, planning, and encouragement.

Pat Somers, who was the office administrator, also proved to be a great listener. When people arrived at the office, or when they called on the phone, Pat exercised great patience and listening abilities. It wasn't her job to remain on the phone, but in that position, she exercised her pastoral gifts very well. Much of the time, phone calls never had to reach the clergy. People could confide in her with great ease. *I should add here that a fantastic amount of pastoral ministry was exercised in the home groups.* Then why is it a standard practice to address one person in the church as the pastor? Or why would one person be addressed as the senior pastor? *Isn't that hierarchical? Isn't that more of an institutional title?*

Even though we tried hard to pattern ourselves after New Testament ministry, I was tired! I spent thirteen years of service at St. James, in which a thriving community had grown and after three years, a lovely and more than adequate facility had been built. When a growing staff became necessary, I was able and more than ready for a sabbatical. I think church members who were teaching at the university understood. But some others sentimentalized my plea for a considerable break. At that point, I didn't need to hear how much I would be missed. After six months, I would be refreshed with new vision.

One morning, after thirteen years at St. James, Pat, quite unusually, walked into my office. With a discretely restrained frown on her face, she told me that the bishop in Victoria wanted to speak with me. Victoria, the capital of British Columbia, is an exceptionally beautiful part of Canada. Some years before, I had been invited to pastor a church there. In my heart, I hoped that one day I would finish my formal ministry in that lovely city. However, I didn't have the slightest sense that it was right at that time.

"This is Bishop Shepherd at Victoria, Charles. The people at Metchosin are insistent that I ask you to meet with them."

"Where on earth is Metchosin, Bishop?"

"Oh, it's only about twenty minutes outside of downtown, Victoria. But it's in a beautiful country area, right on the ocean."

I imagined what it would be: A little old wooden church at the center of an equally small village and dotted with lots of farmhouses. It would be ideal for anyone contemplating a day when he would turn up his toes!

"It's very kind of you, but I don't think it's the place for me."

"But you haven't even seen it yet," Ronald replied. "It's not fair to them if you won't even talk to them."

I wonder if there is a special course for bishops on how to guilt people in the name of God?

The very next week I arrived in Metchosin, a little suburban area of Victoria. Verna didn't come. There was no need for both of us to see it. Since I had been raised in a city, I felt its proximity to Victoria was a positive. But it was very much the way I had thought it to be. The charming, little wooden church was built in 1873, and the hall appeared to have been abandoned by the Romans. But the graveyard was nice! They also had plans to build a new facility. They had very little money but good plans! They had also been planning for years!

After some brief chatter with the council, I dropped my very un-Anglican bombshell! The bombing of Liverpool had been my inspiration on how to cause irreparable damage. It would certainly put the seal of rejection on any invitation directed toward me.

"I am not prepared to spend much of my time on pastoral ministry."

There were frowns all over the room. I could hear the unspoken question: "Then what are you doing here?"

I do remember two people, Bud Boomer and Sharon Hayton, who had wry smiles on their faces.

"My gifts are in evangelism, teaching, and enabling others for ministry. Should we all feel this is a call from God, ministry will become very different from the norm. However, there will emerge a better pastoral ministry, without me."

Bud and June Boomer eventually became very special and supportive friends to Verna and myself. Sharon, after earning a degree at Regent College, Vancouver, succeeded me in my position at Methosin.

The church council had not expected such a reply. It resulted in a prolonged debate. Most of them couldn't imagine a clergyman taking on the role I had described.

"What do we do now?" someone asked.

"Pray," I replied. "I am going back to Calgary!"

And so I did.

"Well, love, there is no way we will be moving to Metchosin. You can relax," I told Verna.

Verna was somewhat relieved because some things were changing in our family.

Kara had been studying at Trinity University, Langley, BC, but was now back in Calgary. Alan, Kara's boyfriend, was looming ever larger in her life. Leah was working in Calgary and becoming serious with Brian. Our son, Mark, was about to enter his final year at high school, but he wasn't too disturbed by the possibility of moving to Victoria. As it turned out, about a year later, I was privileged to conduct a double marriage ceremony for our girls. The service was held in St. James, Calgary.

Often God Speaks Through Others

One day, Jesus healed a paralyzed man not because of his faith but the faith of those who pushed him through the roof (Mark 2:5)! One morning, in the next week, Pat unusually, again, walked into my office! With the same look on her face, she informed me that the bishop in Victoria was on the phone, again.

"I can't believe what's going on in Metchosin, Charles."

"What do you mean?"

"They have never made a unanimous decision in their life. Disagreements in that church are normal. Every person has agreed that you should be their next pastor. I'm very impressed, and I'm offering you the position."

"No you're not," I shouted before he finished his sentence. "Verna hasn't even seen the place. I didn't want to waste her time."

The crafty prelate dug in: "Then it isn't fair to say that it isn't God's will when she hasn't even seen it."

The next week, in the little church at Metchosin, Verna and I were fervently at prayer. We got no answers. We were supposed to give the assembled council an answer in about thirty minutes. I prayed in tongues (Rom. 8:26–27) and immediately received an interpretation. In that word, I remember that a passage of Scripture emerged.

> Forget the former things; do not dwell on the past. See,
> I am doing a new thing! Now it springs up; do you not
> perceive it? (Isa. 43:18–19)

We slumped into the car, not feeling we had an answer to give.

"Wait a minute, Verna. I never use language like that. What do you think it means?"

Immediately, Verna replied, "Here it is."

"Oh, no," I wailed. "This *is* it?"

The perverse irony of this passage is that God was speaking to "my chosen ones"— "Metchosin ones"! (Does God have a perverse sense of humor?) Ten minutes later, we were in Gilbert Nelson's house and looking over a wild and glorious bay of the Strait of Juan de Fuca. Even without such a powerful revelation, how could anyone say no to that!

Three months later, Verna, Mark, and I were at our first service in Metchosin. None of us felt great at all, but we agreed that it was God's will, and that's what mattered. However, my first words of the sermon were: "It's okay. The Second Coming has not arrived; it's just us."

They were very understanding. Indeed, we were to see a number of outstanding miracles in that community. The first one related to the dream of a new church complex.

He Speaks Through Miracles Too

After a year, hardly any more money had appeared. The call of Abraham seemed an appropriate topic for a sermon. What we discovered in Genesis 12 was: (a) God did not give Abraham a blueprint but a direction; (b) the agenda before him had to be God's and not that of Abraham; (c) since it was God's agenda, Abraham could trust that God would provide the resources for his new directions; (d) and most importantly, we learned that the definition of faith (reinforced by Heb. 11:1) is this: *Faith is the positive response to the will of God.*

Faith has nothing to do with positive thought, energy, will, or the ability to persuade God. Questions of the financial or human resources did not fit into the question. If it's not God's will, forget it. *If it is, get on with it!* So I addressed the congregation in this manner: "Is the building of a new complex your idea, or are you laying it on God? After a year of dithering, I need to know. I will not waste my time on a building that is not initiated by God. Please pray very hard. The question for prayer is very simple. Did God order this building, or did we? Two weeks from now, there will be a little piece of blank paper at the door. Just write on it, 'God.' Or you may write, 'We.'"

Two weeks later, the count showed unanimously, "God." Of course, at the door, quite a number of people offered reasons why we shouldn't do anything *yet*.

"If God ordered it, we get on with it *now*."

The next Sunday I asked the people to pray about how much God wanted them to give.

"Don't give a penny more or a penny less than what God has told you."

Then I wrote to the bishop. He must have laughed.

Having been on the diocesan council in Brandon and in Calgary, I knew the strict requirements for erecting new buildings.

"Bishop, we feel that God has called us to erect a new church complex on some new property we have been given. We don't have much money to start with, but God doesn't want us to borrow any. We will hire contractors, but we will also assist them in the construction. If we run out of money, we will put a canvass over the building and leave it there until God provides more money." Because we owned new property, we expected the construction costs to be well over a million dollars. That was an awesome amount for a small congregation in 1988.

Later, the bishop replied, "The council has met and they voted to allow you to go ahead with the project. May God bless you all." (I could see him laughing!) And I expect that the entire council must have wet themselves with laughter!

Often we felt like Nehemiah and his fellow workers. We had one hand on the tools and one raised to Yahweh Jireh (God our Provider, Gen. 22:14). Once, we really were at the point where we had to stop building. That just left us another hand to raise toward God. However, someone (whom nobody in the church knew) many years before had returned to England from Metchosin. She died and left the church $100,000. Her family in England contested it. We said we would not.

"You just pray to God about what He would have you do, and we will not go to court over your decision."

The building went on. The result was, after about two and a half years of steady building, and not a few little miracles, God had proven how faith actually works. One Sunday in 1991, we began a service in the crowded little church. Then we filed out singing songs of praise accompanied by my acoustic guitar. We lit a candle from one on the old church altar, and off we went.

One quarter of a mile later on our windy walk, we paraded into the new church building. The candle was still alight, and on that day, *we were completely debt free!* The day we walked into the new building, every cent had been paid. God had provided, just as He had promised. From our lighted candle, we lit the two that were on the brand new table of the Lord, and we finished our service of praise and thanksgiving. It was not the only miracle we witnessed there.

You Have to Find a Place to Dig First

Gill Armstrong, the wife of Mike, our building overseer, was on the phone. They lived in a high and hilly district of Metchosin country. Not surprisingly, water was a problem for them and their neighbors. "We have a difficult decision to make. On five occasions, we have tried to drill for water, but we have always had poor results. A relative has left us a little money; we wonder whether we should risk another attempt. Most of our neighbors continue to have water delivered."

Verna and I went up to their place. We discussed the problem with Gill and Mike, and then we did what they had asked us to do.

"Where would be the easiest place for the drillers to work?" I asked.

Mike told me that it would be at the bottom of their property, right beside the gate.

We walked to the gate and then held hands in prayer. While we were holding hands, I believe God told me what the prayer should be: "Lord, two hundred feet below, in the name of Jesus, we command the ground to move and the water to gush forth." (Forth?) Amen!

Three days later, Gill phoned again.

"The drillers have got down to seventy-five feet, and we are getting water. It's running about eight gallons an hour. That's not very good."

"What did we pray a few days ago?" I asked.

"That the water would gush two hundred feet below," Gill replied.

"Well?" I gently reminded her.

"Okay," she said as she put down her phone.

Later in the afternoon, she was on the phone again.

"We've got water all over the place. It's amazing!"

Many years later (when we left Metchosin), Mike and Gill were still supplying water to their neighbors!

We have noticed that when God has reminded us to take seriously principles by which the apostolic church operated, signs and wonders often accompanied the principles. (See Acts 5:12, 14.) *For the apostle Paul, the authenticity of the gospel and of his position in the church rested on a vindication given by signs and wonders* (2 Cor. 12:12). I cannot see that the apostolic church was only casually interested in showing this. For example, the apostle Paul was concerned that the church in Corinth (which he founded) had not gone very far.

> My speech and my proclamation were not with plausible words of wisdom, but with a demonstration of the Spirit and of power, so that your faith might not rest on human wisdom [i.e., like the philosophy of the Gentile Greeks] but on the power of God. (1 Cor. 2:4–5)

In other words, you were persuaded and converted not by clever arguments but by signs and wonders that confirmed the reality of the message (Mark 16:20, John 14:11).

"I have heard clergy preach about faith all my life, but this is the first time I have ever seen it at work," my doctor, a member of the congregation, said when he was changed by God's intervention of signs and wonders.

Truly, God was telling us that we were being blessed because, in obedience, we followed His will. But the apostle Paul realized that without further discipleship, the Corinthian Christians would remain as babes in the faith (1 Cor. 3:1–2). Miraculously, erecting a new building was just the beginning sign of making believing disciples at Metchosin. I can't just write about techniques and teaching that help build up a community of believers. That's not the biblical way. It was often signs and wonders that drew attention to the integrity and power of the gospel.

CHAPTER 5

Back to the Future

Burned Out in Ministry

A young pastor admitted to his overseer that he was feeling burned out in his new ministry.

"Burned out?" the overseer replied. "I never thought you were on fire!"

For some reason, this complaint is more common than we realize. However, Reginald Bibby tells us that in the USA since about 1990, church attendance amongst older baby boomers has changed.

+ 42% had remained involved continuously ("Loyalists")

+ 22% had dropped out and returned ("Returnees")

+ the remaining 36% were still uninvolved ("Dropouts")

And in Canada, as of about 1990, "these younger boomers were exhibiting attendance levels very similar to those of the older boomers when the latter were the same age in the 1970s and 1980s."[7] In simpler terms, in North America we have not experienced an explosion of church

---

7   Bibby, Reginald. W, *Unknown Gods*, (Stoddart Publishing Co., Toronto, 1993) p.15

attendance, even if some churches are growing. Yet often when I ask clergy how they are doing, a surprising percentage will answer, "Oh, I am very busy."

"But that is not the question," I reply.

Why is this response so common? One of the problems here is of *job description*. When a congregation rises over the barrier of two hundred in attendance, it is more likely that a job description has been worked out. Both the pastor and the congregation have an agreed-upon understanding of expectations but not always. Sometimes the absurd expectation that the pastor should continue being involved in or even controlling everything still lingers on. In smaller congregations, the problems of ill-defined expectations become more apparent.

With a poor job description, the pastor is not given any freedom to say no to requests (or demands) from the membership. Everybody seems to have a right to require a smile, a nod, and legs to any request. A big problem looms here. When clergy confide in me that they are exhausted, I will often ask the questions:

+ Exhausted in doing what?

+ Who said you were supposed to do all those things?

+ What do you and the council see as your spiritual gifting?

+ How are you released to major in the areas you are gifted?

+ How are you freed up to encourage the church leadership in their ministries?

Expectations of Pastors

A more common problem in those smaller churches is that the pastor really does do all the things that are needed. The standard expectation of a pastor is that he or she is always available, at any time, to do whatever the members require. I am not talking about tasks that come under the *volunteer* category. What I mean is that he or she conducts the major part of the service, preaches, visits members in the hospital, follows up with new people, visits those on the church list, administers the use of church

facilities, recruits new members, teaches all the courses, takes leadership
in fundraising, and counsels when people need help. The pastor is the *jack
of all trades*. And even if it's a small church, *who said the pastor is equipped
for all these ministries?*

Whether, or not he is, the faithful pastor tries it all anyway. The
reality is, nobody really knows how hard he or she is really working. *He
may even be doing more work just looking busy!* He may be doing more work
than he should. Maybe he should not be doing much of what he is doing.
So long as he remains good friends with a few leaders, then everyone
thinks he is busy doing very important things. *For many churches, there
isn't an effective process of accountability or of encouragement.* This may be
an oversimplification. The fact is, in a smaller church, when the same
person does the basic ministry, the pastor often fills in time with jobs
that should normally be done by others. In the smaller church, for the
work that is being done, is there need for a full-time pastor? And in the
larger church, the pastor may easily become absorbed in ministries that
are not his. In these days of declining membership (in mainline churches)
should the majority of a pastor's time be spent on visiting?

It is in this no-win situation that the pastor may seem to have the need
to tell the congregation how busy he is. And as long as the congregation
accepts that the pastor is busy, then they are all happy. He may be! Is
that what it's really all about, Alfie? *Frustration, improper expectations,
poor methods of accountability, and ineffective training* are the main causes
for burnout. That young pastor complaining to his overseer was placed
into a church that ministered in an old but anachronistic (of a by-gone
but unworkable) system.

Any church may clothe itself in a wineskin that hasn't effectively
been prepared for ministry. But churches, large or small, can quite easily,
with good resources, enter into a process of *disciple making*. Even a small
church can expect to have a pastor who is equipped to enable a process
of disciple making. Even the pastor of a small church can harness outside
resources to help with the process. Even a small church can expect its
pastor to prioritize his own personal life in commitment to Jesus, to his
family, and third, to the church.

It is here that we may reconsider how we use our seminary personnel.

Why should those learned people remain, for years, huddled behind those hallowed halls?

What if their major tasks were in teaching and training entire groups of church leaders in those important academic and practical leadership subjects? Of course, I am assuming that the teachers also have the experience to train. Maybe these important resource people should be expected to spend sabbaticals on the job and in real life-changing situations. Maybe experienced trainers from other churches or denominations can be utilized. Imagine how this may change the shape of preparation for ordination! Married people with children and few financial resources could now respond to their call.

Church Positions and Gifting

Many of today's seminaries insist on preparing students primarily in a feminine style. Even with male teachers? Yes, even with male teachers! Of course, I am speaking in natural terms. The female psyche more generally *looks inward* to a nurturing, supportive, cooperative, and protective focus. That doesn't mean to say that women can't possess a dominant outward focus. Of course they can. But in general and natural terms, it is the male (as the historical provider) who exercises the dominant focus of looking *beyond the home*. (In the West of today, that is not always the situation.)

Usually, the male focus, as a leader in the church, more naturally looks to the world beyond the local church community. He may more naturally look to a much larger environment in need of the gospel of Jesus. By the very nature of the word, we may say that the apostolic nature of the gospel has a primary outward focus. However, in real terms, I remember, even when I was in college, our practical training was largely taken up in counseling, listening skills, visiting, etc. We were being taught to be chaplains but certainly not apostolic enablers.

APOSTOLIC OUTWARD FOCUS

THE SENDING FATHER. John 3:16 God sent His Son
|
THE SENDING SON. Acts 1:8. Sent Out the Apostolic Community
|
THE SENDING AND EMPOWERING SPIRIT. Acts 2:1-3. Sent by the Father, Promised by the Son, Anoints and Empowers the Apostolic Community that Gathered at Pentecost
|
THE APOSTOLIC COMMUNITY. Focused in the Twelve, sent on a Ministry of Reconciliation. 2Cor.5:19, Acts 5: 12-14
|
THE MINISTRY OF APOSTLESHIP. Eph.4:11. Set Apart by Local Church Congregations to establish new communities of the Faith Locally and in the World. Acts 13:1-3, Titus 1:5

There are a great many more women offering themselves for ordination today. Indeed, in my own Calgary Synod, I was the one who presented the paper in favor of women's ordination. It is not a question of rights. In theological terms, there is no reason why a woman, if called by God, should not be ordained. The question is one not of men versus women but the place of each in the whole apostolic schema. The outward focus must be seen to be the primary focus of Christian life (John 3:16—that is a countercultural direction). The fact is that both apostolic and pastoral directions are important.

The problems lie when inward directions become dominant. Sorry to digress, but I had to start laying foundations for the predominance of apostolic principles. We really do have to look at questions not so much of ordination *but of leadership within the church.* Clearly the person who takes the leading role in any church community must have a *dominant outward focus.* Normally that would be a male person, *but not always.* God desires to call the best person for overall leadership; sometimes that person is a woman. (Historically, we may easily see that the systems don't always produce the one who is called by God.) What state would Israel have been in had not God raised up women like Deborah and Esther. What state would the New Testament church have found itself without the amazing ministries of women? As I noted at the beginning of this chapter, the Western church is largely in decline and mainly because we have reversed our focus to one that looks inward. Do our titles suggest this?

At the local level, the head of a local church system is usually the paid professional. He or she may bear the title of pastor, priest, minister, rector, or some other institutional or denominational tag. Whatever the title may be, the apostolic *focus seems to be very rare in today's mainline churches*. It's no wonder these churches are declining. Evangelical seminaries and Bible colleges often fare differently. Despite the fact that many mainline church leaders claim to have better training, the focus of Evangelical churches are certainly more apostolic. The results speak for themselves.

Do I Get Full-Time Pay?

In these days, when it is difficult to find well-trained clergy for a small church, such persons may not be able to expect full-time employment. It is not easy to find well-trained clergy for a small church position. In this Western climate, *part-time clergy are becoming more abundant*. But this seemingly sad situation may be turned around to appear like a first-century church in business! (It could result with a part-time leader being called according to his gifting in enabling). The apostle Paul gladly accepted the situation, even though he had the right to expect more (1 Cor. 9:15). Obviously, in his missionary situation, he felt he could witness more effectively by working alongside the average working person. The witness of being alongside others in their daily life may be very effective for the *pastor* and those he serves.

"I can't see myself ever going back to a full-time paid position."

David had given up his full-time position in a Victoria church in order to free up resources for outside mission. To his surprise, he realized his world had become the world of the church. He thought that he was part of the church in the world. "I am now much more in touch with the world. I appreciate more easily what our church members have to face. And my witness has become much more perceptive and meaningful. I really do learn so much from the people who work with me." The same thing is now being said by our son, Mark. He was ordained in a mainline Protestant denomination.

Once a training process of apostolic direction is in place, it becomes an expectation that the ordained person will spend the majority of his time *affirming, encouraging, and training* in the ministries to which God has called the people.

In my first charge at Snow Lake, Manitoba, most people actually liked me! But the church people liked me even more when they didn't have to pay me! As I began working for the local mining company twenty-five hundred feet underground, some expected me to continue as if I were being paid by them.

"What a wonderful pastor! He is glad to work another eight hours a day." But who said a clergyman should do all the hospital visiting? Is he the best preacher in the church? Where are those who are called and equipped for pastoral ministries? A bigger question is, who trains them? Isn't this what Ephesians 4 is all about?

> It was he who gave some to be apostles, some to be prophets, some to be evangelists, and some to be pastors and teachers, to prepare God's people for works of service, so that the body of Christ my be built up ... (Eph. 4:11)

I saw a similar confusion of roles ably demonstrated when I was once asked to conduct a church conference on the subject of church ministry. Naturally, I had drawn the congregation to a consideration of Ephesians 4:11 for today. Fitzroy was a very good pastor who enabled members of the church to do ministries very well. The only problem was that most of the congregation had not yet begun to think of ministry beyond the four walls of the church building! *They were mostly churchy ministries.* I ventured to throw out some questions.

"Who are the apostles in this church?" I asked.

"Fitzroy," was the immediate reply. He looked disappointed!

"Who are the prophets in this church?" I asked.

"Fitzroy," they shouted. His shoulders drooped!

"Who are the evangelists in this church?" I asked.

"Would that be Fitzroy?" they quizzically replied.

His eyes rolled!

"Who are the pastors?"

"That must be Fitzroy," some shouted. He was visibly frustrated!

"Who are the teachers?"

By this time, I was beginning to feel like a twit for asking!

"We do have Sunday school teachers," was the slow but puzzled reply.

"But I know Fitzroy," I retorted. "And I know that the Holy Spirit most definitely hasn't gifted him with all those abilities."

They agreed! *But they didn't know where they really fitted into this exotic-looking picture! And who was this little twit challenging them to think bigger?* I asked them to think of the meaning of the following passage on gifts, but in their own context of purpose:

> All these [gifts] are the work of the one and same Spirit, and he gives them to each one, just as he determines. (1 Cor. 12:11)

What we have lightly observed is that the Holy Spirit offers His gifts to *all* the people of God in one region of activity (1 Cor. 12:4–6, 11). Of course, these gifts are much more likely to be discovered and affirmed in a church that deliberately offers a course of *Growing in Christ* or *Alpha* or something comparable. But also, the gifts required for effective ministry in a much larger area cannot be found in one congregation. And in one congregation, all the gifts required for ministry are not allotted to one person. These gifts are recognized, nurtured, and affirmed in the local community of the faith. In each context, a system of enabling and affirmation is encouraged through which all the believers are freed and enabled to function. *There are titles for these ministries, but they are not institutional titles. They are titles that are related to spiritual gifting.*

For example, a title such as *archbishop* is an institutional title; it has no biblical precedent. It is usually interpreted to mean the first among bishops. (A title beginning with a word like *arch*, meaning first, becomes the opposite of the servant ministry that Jesus taught. See the washing of the feet in John 13. Also see how Jesus reacted to the presumptuous request of James and John's mother; see Matt. 20:20–23 and Mark

9:35.) There are other hierarchical titles indicating a status within the institution (i.e., archbishop, cardinal, metropolitan). And what about senior pastor? Is the senior pastor really the most gifted in pastoral ministries? What have such titles to do with spiritual gifting?

In Ephesians 4:11, people who are given gifts to church plant are engaged in an *apostolic ministry*; they are *apostles*. Those who are clearly gifted in leading people to Christ are those engaged in a ministry of *evangelism*. Those who are gifted in counseling, or who care for those with problems, are engaged in *pastoral ministry*, etc. They are not jobs for one person to do! Nor could one person train others in all these ministries.

In the Ephesian church, there were five broad ministries identified by Paul. (The other two are teachers and prophets.) With support and training in their ministries, the apostle Paul said that leaders in such areas would be called upon.

> To equip the saints for the work of ministry, for building
> up the body of Christ. (Eph. 4:12 NRSV)

That is why we discovered in Calgary that trained ministers could be raised up from within the local commission. Actually, I learned of this process more effectively when I began to understand the power of a *group-based church*. However, I also had to learn what it means to be *an apostolic church in name and nature*. Maybe we have used the term *apostolic* much too lightly. Maybe we have to examine how it was used in the first-century church.

An Apostolic Church; What's That?

If we were to ask almost any Christian congregation the question, "Are you an apostolic church?" most probably, every one of them would say, "Yes. Of course we are."

"What makes you an apostolic church?" we may persist.

"Well, we say the Apostles' Creed, and we try to follow what the apostles believed and practiced."

That's not a bad answer, but isn't there more to it than that? When I started to look beyond mainline denominations for ministry definitions, I realized that there are at least five major areas that are fundamentally apostolic. You may think I'm pressing it, but I'm biblically convinced that a congregation should be working on all five of them—that is, if they really want to be serious about *making disciples* in the apostolic tradition. (Everyone needs some tradition, and some is really necessary!)

Who wants to go back to horse and buggy days? Not me; I like my little car and my cell phone, and I also like to watch TV! But Bob Dylan was right: "The times, they are a-changin'." We're in an entirely different world than that of New Testament days. *Remarkably, we are in an entirely different world than we were just twenty years ago!*

The new world of physics, philosophy, and other disciplines provides ample evidence for that. Exclusive allegiance to principles of the Enlightenment period is now sort of old-fashioned! *And that fact alone should awaken the church!* Actually, it's very clear that twenty years is just about the length of time that cultural values and directions survive in the West anyway. Even so, George Hunsberger suggests that the values of the Church have already become domesticated. "It has arisen comfortably from a set of cultural values that have uncritically been allowed to shape the scope of mission before us."[8] What this means is that the church has to meet the unbelieving world in different ways than before. No longer do we have Christendom rights, but we can demonstrate a superior way.

Does this mean that the faith also changes? No, it doesn't!

Then, do we have to look backward in order to move forward? Actually, in some ways we must, but not to copy but to translate the past (Gal. 6:14). The reasons are really quite simple:

- God's plan and purposes for His creation have never changed (Isa. 46:9–10).

- The purpose of God's community has never changed.

- The essential nature and needs of humanity have never changed.

---

8   George R. Hunsberger and Craig Van Gelder, eds. *Church Between Gospel and Culture.* (Grand Rapids, MI: Eerdmans, 1996), 5.

+ Basic apostolic *principles* are astonishingly relevant for today.

In the light of social changes in this rapid techno-communication age, we may easily see that *this generation is not a people of memory!*

The limited vocabulary of a texting generation has often made it ignorant of language that speaks of mystery, transcendence, and the importance of community. But we have to meet people there for them to move into significant and mature areas of discipleship.

In some ways, it's not a new situation. The ancient Hebrews experienced this problem about thirty-two hundred years ago! In just one generation, a people of common memory and language had lost it! In just one generation, after the people of Israel moved into the Promised Land, the writer(s) of Judges makes this observation:

> After that whole generation had been gathered to their
> fathers, another generation grew up, who knew neither
> the Lord nor what he had done for Israel. (Judges 2:10)

Isn't it amazing what can happen when an emerging culture refuses to learn from history and its past principles? *What we do today will probably last for just one generation!* The next generation also has to witness and translate (not compromise) the gospel into their age. If that doesn't happen, then the next generation repeats the lament.

> In those days Israel had no king; everyone did as he saw
> fit. (Judges 21:25)

As in the first century, the church now treads on virgin territory for the gospel of Jesus Christ. Christendom is dead. Therefore, no longer may we expect easy passage into the systems of our culture. We have to earn it! So we go back to the time of the apostles to rediscover *apostolic principles for every time and age.* These principles, if we are to remain *authentically Christian, remain nonnegotiable.* Indeed, we are to see that the following characteristics are absolutely essential to the entire meaning of apostolicity.

CHAPTER 6

Five Nonnegotiable Apostolic Principles

Quite deliberately, I use the term *nonnegotiable* for a very important reason. And it's not to say that if you don't agree with me, you are on the way to hell. No, it's because your church may not be at the point where it can accept all five principles. If that's the case, then you will certainly have problems with this process. In fact, all five principles are needed in order to arrive at and work with the biblical system that's being proposed. Once I had to tell a pastor I could no longer help him. He was trying to pick and choose from the materials of the Timothy Institute process. Taking dabs here and there just won't work. But heartily, I do wish you God's blessing if you can't go through a tried and tested process of making disciples. (Maybe the resources on my web page will be helpful: www.timothyministry.ca.)

First: Apostolic Belief

That is the passing on of the essential good news that was given to the twelve apostles by Jesus. In their worship services, most historic churches include the reading of the Bible, and certain historic creeds, such as the Apostles' Creed or the Nicene Creed. *We practice what we believe; it's not the other way around!* But it's not just a matter of saying the right words. I'll repeat this important verse of Scripture.

> I felt I had to write and urge you to contend for the faith
> that was once for all entrusted to the saints. (Jude 3)

In other words, the Bible records the story of God's revelation to us. The story is about the experience of God's revelation and one experienced by an historical community. As predicted in the Old Testament, it is fully revealed to us in Jesus (John 14:9). He is the First and the Last (Rev. 1:17). He is the Word of God from before the foundation of the world (John 1:1). That is an essential tradition. It is a vital principle. We don't have to interpret every word of the Bible in literal form. (There were many literary devices used in the Bible.) However, we do have to accept that the Bible is our ultimate authority in revealing God's will and purpose for His creation (Isa. 46:10).

The first words of the Apostles' Creed, "I believe," come from the Greek word *pisteuo*. That word is not about some kind of intellectual consent but a *life commitment to what it says (even because that historic experience is bigger than mine).*

"You and I could stand alongside these two bishops, and word for word, we could all repeat the words of the Apostles' Creed. But as you know, those two bishops would not mean what we say or what the church has meant for nearly two thousand years." I was writing to a godly and leading person of a national church. My concern was that he was saying, "So long as we can say the creeds together and don't change the written doctrines of the church, we could agree that we were all in unity."

To me, that statement was no more meaningful than washing deck chairs on the *Titanic*. It was no more meaningful than repeating the oaths of a local service club.

"Our unity is not seen by mouthing words of an ecclesiastical club. It has to be seen in a person who is absolute truth (John 14:6). *And that person is Jesus Christ.*" Our unity is in the person of Jesus (Eph. 4:15–16). It was not for me to judge (Matt. 7:1), but *according to the public statements of those two bishops,* they did not appear to have a basic and personal experience of Jesus as Savior and Lord. In other words, they did not demonstrate the basic motivation that propels people to say the creeds. Their language and experience rarely seemed to concur with the historic experience of the apostolic church.

Quite honestly, the faith these two bishops were openly espousing was much more their own than that of the historic church. The apostle Paul summed up this present-day situation like this:

> I am astonished that you are so quickly deserting the one who called you by the grace of Christ and are turning to a different gospel-which is really no gospel at all. Evidently some people are throwing you into confusion and are trying to pervert the gospel of Christ. (Gal. 1:6–7)

The apostle Peter echoes the same sentiment:

> But there were also false prophets among the people, just as there will be false teachers among you. They will secretly introduce destructive heresies, even denying the sovereign Lord who bought them-bringing swift destruction on themselves. (2 Pet. 2:1)

The apostolic faith is recorded as the community teaching of the revelation and experience of a relationship with God, through Christ, and expressed in loving concern for others. Therefore, the Christian faith is not about the teaching of a dead carpenter but the experience of the resurrected Savior. Only a living Savior is able to raise the dead to life. "I am the resurrection and the life. Those who believe in me, even though they die, will live" (John 11:25). Thousands of Christians every year die for the name of Jesus. They don't die for an ecclesiastical institution but for the Person of Jesus Christ. Peter Brierly quotes from *The World Churches Handbook* (edited by Timothy Bradshaw): "Since 1980, about 80,000 people are brought to Christ every day. Astoundingly, about 20,000 of them are in China and other Bamboo countries."[9] Quite remarkably, the church in China suffers great persecution, and it's not yet legal to hold large Christian meetings in China. *Consequently, this phenomenal growth is being made possible by an almost exclusive emphasis on the home-based church!*

The fact is, while mainline churches of the West are watering down the gospel in their haste to act as chaplains to the culture, Christians of the global south speak and live prophetically to their cultures. They also are in need of transcendence, hope, and meaning. There is a major difference in changing water to wine (John 2) and reducing wine to water! It's mustard seed Christianity in China. The Christian faith is represented in a small percentage of the 1.2 billion population, but it's growing! *It speaks of lives that have been transformed, not only through a tradition of right teaching, but by their introduction to a life of right relationships! They know life through Jesus!*

That is the faith for which almost all of the apostles died. It's the faith for which thousands are dying every day. It's not about spirituality; it's all about the one who is the truth. It is this faith that joins us together in one body. It's not in a religion where we find unity; it's in a person—*Jesus Christ*.

> Built upon the foundation of the apostles and prophets,
> with Christ Jesus himself as the cornerstone. (Eph. 2:20)

Second: A Heart for the Broken and the Lost

I was in Jerusalem and standing at the Western Wall. With both hands on the ancient stones (some call it the Wailing Wall), my eyes were closed as I prayed for the peace of Jerusalem. I was glad to be there. I really didn't have any sense of an emotion, but I prayed also for the Jewish people. And then I started to pray in tongues.

In a matter of ten seconds, I was bawling uncontrollably. After I composed myself, I asked the Lord, "What was that all about?"

---

9 Timothy Ed Bradshaw, *Grace and Truth in the Secular Age.* (Grand Rapids, MI: Wm. B.Eeerdmans, 1998), 15.

Suddenly I felt I had been privileged to enter into the heart of God. I began to understand what God felt concerning His ancient people, Israel. What a privilege! Somehow I believe this story captures something of the heart we must have for all those who are lost and without Jesus. We are not called to fill pews but to present Christ to those whose hearts are empty without Him. When churches enter into a process of evangelism, their goal is not *church growth* but personal salvation. In that order, churches tend to get filled anyway. The question is, *do we really believe that people are eternally lost without Jesus?* By entering into the heart of God, we develop a passion for the lost and broken. In other words, there is little point in evangelism if this passion does not come first.

I have been in many situations where people, in the name of evangelism, feel they are doing well or terrible when the criterion becomes the occupancy level of the church building. Jesus never told His followers to go into the world to fill churches but to make disciples. Why is that? It's because of the heart of God. He gave His only Son in order to have a relationship with the entire population of the world. Of course, God grieves when some choose not to enter into that kind of intimacy (1 Tim. 2:4)—that's the nature of freedom—but He rejoices over every single person who enters into a relationship that is eternal (1 John 5:11–13).

"God has called me to help build a big community here."

"I will be very happy if I am still in this little church twenty-five years from now."

These were the paradoxical answers given to me by two different pastors. I had asked them what they felt was their purpose in their church. Now I happen to know both of those pastors have a personal love for Jesus, and they want to share it with others. What I wanted to hear from them were the words, "I have a love and passion for all those who do not know Jesus."

That's what John 3:16 is all about. Both of those pastors would agree that evangelism is not about filling pews. But for some reason, many people have the need to articulate this passion for the lost in some sort of institutional way. The New Testament is clear.

> For the Son of Man came to seek and to save what was lost. (Luke 19:10)

> For God did not send his Son into the world to condemn the world, but to save the world through him. (John 3:17)

The writer of 2 Peter puts it very beautifully:

> The Lord is not slow in keeping his promise, as some understand slowness. He is patient with you, not wanting anyone to perish, but everyone to come to repentance. (2 Pet. 3:9)

We know that God doesn't want any to perish (1Tim.2:4) but not everyone will be saved. That would be a total denial of God's creation principle of personal freedom to choose. Anyway, a relationship of love could not exist without the element of such freedom.

There is often a great deal of talk about the word *evangelism*, but sometimes the talk actually is dominated by the notion of *church growth*. There is nothing particularly wrong with church growth, and there is nothing wrong with hearing how we may attract and keep new people. *But we must always put the biblical priority first in our motivation and thinking.* We were commanded to make disciples long before we ever built churches. God, by His very nature, is a relational God, and that is what He seeks in those made after His image. People are lonely until they relate to the Original.

What other religion, in the entire history of the world can say all this? What other religion can say something so simple as this: *What God intended for His creatures, He also rescued for His purposes.*

Therefore, in the process of disciple making, the initial goal is to raise disciples to love Jesus so much that evangelism is a normal activity and goal of every single day. That is why the most important basic component of *making disciples* is bringing church people and converts to a lively and intimate relationship with Jesus.

If we are truly into the heart of God, then our primary purpose is to bring people into that relationship that is eternally restored by God. God did it; we receive it. We are not saved by our decision for God but His decision for us. We are not called to work for it but to live in it!

> For it is by grace you have been saved, through faith- and this not from yourselves, it is the gift of God—not by works so that no one can boast. (Eph. 2:8–9)

> Work out your salvation with fear and trembling. (Phil. 2:12)

This latter verse is a far cry from working *for* our salvation but working it *out*.

For a variety of reasons we need to be very careful not to repeat the mistakes of the past. For example, there is a great need today, particularly in mainline churches, to be acceptable to the culture. Old Israel did the same thing. *They focused in on themselves and forgot the major purposes that God had for them* (Jer. 32:22–23). The call of Abraham shows clearly that His offspring were intended to have a universal mission. Through them, the world could be well blessed with the presence and provisions of God (Gen.12:1–3). *God's revelation often took a lowly position.* Hence, from the heart of a loving Father came a plea to return to a relationship of love extending to the world.

Then God, instead of sending prophets and teachers, expressed the utmost love in coming down to us Himself. *God came down to us because we could not reach up to Him.*

Only God Himself could restore a lost humanity back to the essential relationships of Eden (Heb. 1:1–3). In human form, God was reconciling the world to Himself (2 Cor. 5:19). And it was all because of love (John 3:16)! *The New Testament is therefore about a seeking God who will go to the ends of the earth to find the lost.* That's a comment made by D. M. Baillie. He quotes Claude Montefiore, a former Jew who became a Christian bishop. Montefiore saw a striking difference between the Old and New Testaments. The God of Jesus was "a seeking God, whose very nature it is to go the whole way into the wilderness in quest of man."[10] That's the very heart of Christ's ministry; the ministry of the Good Shepherd (John 10:1–10).

Of course, the gospel of Jesus is both *spiritual and social*, and they really can't be separated. That's because we are whole beings, body, soul, and spirit. Sometimes people of mainline churches think they have the whole gospel. And sometimes people of evangelical persuasions think it is they who have it all. It's a matter of where most energy and resources are spent. One group may spend their efforts toward the broken while another may concentrate on the lost. Jesus doesn't give us a choice. Note the wholeness with which Jesus is concerned.

> I tell you the truth, no one can see the kingdom of God unless he is born again. (John 3:3)

> Lord, when did we see you hungry or thirsty or a stranger or needing clothes or sick or in prison, and did not help you? He will reply, "I tell you the truth, whatever you did not do for one of the least of these, you did not do for me." (Matt. 25:44–45)

In the first instance, it's easy to see that the work required in bringing a person into an eternal relationship with God comes from above; *it is the work of the Holy Spirit.* (The Greek word *anothen*, sometimes interpreted as *born again*, is best understood to mean, *born from above*.) In the second instance, *we are working out the ministry of salvation* in the outward signs that the kingdom is partly signed. In other words, through the church, there are signs that, in the New Creation, there is no more hunger or loneliness or thirst or nakedness or sickness or self-centeredness (Rev. 7).

The fact is, today a neo-evangelicalism is growing. This movement centers on the meaning of both gospel aspects. Indeed, where I live in Calgary, the most outstanding *evangelical churches* are equally concerned with both gospel emphases. Of course, there are some mainline churches that have always understood the importance of this balance. Sadly,

---

10 D. M. Baillie, *God Was in Christ.* (London: Faber and Faber Ltd., 1961), 63–64.

however, in statements of purpose, all too many mainline churches are now stating their desire to help the broken alone. It's a gospel of justice. But whose justice? (God's justice and righteousness go together, Isa.16:5.) If a church membership doesn't experience a living relationship with God in the work of the Spirit, then what other reason have they for existence than working for justice in brokenness?

Clearly, the foundations of apostolic belief are paramount and stand as our authority for what we do. We minister according to what we believe. However, *it isn't enough simply to have all the right belief in place* (James 2:26). To claim apostolic belief without the apostolic heart of God is a denial of the very nature of the gospel! We aren't interested in creating big churches through successful techniques, but we are to be so in love with God that we burst with the desire to share in His heart's desires.

Third: A Primary Outward Focus In Determining Ministries, Goals, and Priorities

Once, when I went to a party, after a while, I said to the host, "This is a boring party. I think I'll leave." He replied, "Oh, well, that will help!"

With whom would you rather spend most of your time? Would it be with someone who is always looking inward and whose conversation naturally revolves around him? Or would you prefer to spend time with someone who mostly looks outside of his own world and whose conversation takes on broader perspectives? Most people would agree that the people they choose as friends are much more likely to have an outward focus. They are often a tonic. Apart from biblical imperatives in this direction, isn't it more likely that newcomers to your church will remain with you when they see you as a community that reaches out and has goals and a method for achieving them?

I want to suggest that, by the very nature of God's Trinitarian life, our God looks out to *otherness*. In that sense, it's not hard to understand that in His nature, *He is the sending God.*

During that year or even more, as Verna and I trudged from one church to another, we would pay close attention to the church bulletin. *First,* we looked for the *statement of the church's mission.* How much did its vision look out beyond the interior life of the congregation? *Second,* in terms of all *the activity,* how much of it reached beyond the needs of the church membership? *Third,* in terms of the *financial resources,* what percentage was spent on the needs of the congregation compared with that spent on the needs of those beyond the church?

> I have other sheep that are not of this sheep pen. I must bring them also. They too will listen to my voice, and there shall be one flock and one shepherd. (John 10:16)

Fourth, was it a good experience to have been there? Did we meet with God? Would we look forward to going there again next week? Is all this too much to ask? Of course, I am speaking about worshippers who want an experience of joy because the worship brought them right into the presence of God.

It is absolutely vital that the contemporary church (especially in the West) learns to shift toward this primary outward focus. In a *me-centered* culture, churches become easily preoccupied with the wants of their membership. Clearly there are real needs in the community that must be met. However, all too often the proportion of the resources of time, energy, and money spent on the needs of the membership far outweigh that which is spent for the sake of others.

Often during a teaching conference, I would likely ask a congregation to test itself in the following manner: *"What percentage of all the time, money, and other resources is spent for the benefit of yourselves, and what percentage is spent for the benefit of others?"*

When I began to take seriously the meaning of a group-based church (i.e., not a program church with groups but a church whose entire life emanates from a group-based structure), I noticed a clear and exciting process. When the primary focus of a church is outward looking, then the inner quality of fellowship, sharing, and support actually increases.

For example, at one congregation where I was teaching the principles of a group-based church, this program-based community already had groups working, as part of the process. They began to understand implications of the reality that "a program-based church produces 40-50 percent of non-active members."[11] According to the same commentator, "This kind of church will release only about 15 percent of its people into seriously committed ministries."[12] Eventually we arrived at the point where we could test out the group event. Later, one of the leaders was very excited. He told me of what had happened at their session. "We followed the entire process of the session, just as you suggested. It works!"

Now this was a group that had already been meeting for years but based around the usual Bible study. "One guy has been in our group for years. We have never been able to get him to say anything. We followed your suggestions at the beginning, and he started to talk. After a short while, he just burst out, like an unstoppable flood. The result was that we had the best time of ministry we have ever had." Clearly the idea that the quality of fellowship diminishes with an outward focus is really not true; at least it isn't true *when the event is done properly.*

However, I have discovered that when the focus is reversed, the outward imperatives really do diminish. Of course, it may be obvious by now, but a heart for the lost and the broken will rarely merit a primary focus if there is not an ongoing process of discipleship in the church. Unfortunately, the above-mentioned church was not at all ready to emphasize an outward focus as its primary goal. Not only did it express disunity in adopting the group-based church, but it just plodded on for a long time. Eventually the entire congregation fell apart and totally disbanded.

To well-meaning churches, one of the dangers to be avoided is that their style and methods become very image and culturally focused. Not surprisingly, then, such churches lose their distinctive message of holiness and sacrifice within the culture. *Is it possible to gain a vast congregation and lose our own soul (Mark 8:36)?*

The churches that make me the most uncomfortable are those that are the most comfortable! What message would be given if the church billboard displayed the following text?

---

11   Ralph Neighbour, *Where Do We Go from Here?* (Houston, TX: Touch Publications, 1990), 49.

12   Ibid., 49.

> If you are looking for a comfortable
> church, this isn't it!

I feel a need to say something about pastoral ministries within a church community. Henry Nouwen once wrote a book entitled *The Wounded Healers.* Of course, as he so wonderfully demonstrated, we are all wounded people. None of us come to ministry as a completed project. And that is why we must say that we enter into ministry not when we feel we are ready but when we are bringing with us our weaknesses and dependence upon the Holy Spirit.

When the late second-century Tertullian challenged a Roman official with the words, "See how these Christians love one another," he was illustrating how Christians act in sharp contrast to the self-centered Roman community. Although the early church saw phenomenal growth, nevertheless, it was also a caring and supportive community.

> There were no needy persons among them. For from time to time those who owned lands or houses sold them, brought the money from the sales and put it at the apostles' feet, and it was distributed to anyone as he had need. (Acts 4:34)

> And day by day the Lord added to their number those who were being saved. (Acts 2:47)

The same principles should be applied to the question of mission. Overseas or local, is not the principle the same? Mission is both. When our primary focus lies beyond ourselves, we appreciate and support the fine work of organizations such as World Vision or Iris Ministries. But giving to missions far away is no excuse for not making our priorities at the local level. That's where the group-based church becomes a wonderful avenue for getting mission and pastoral work in perspective.

Fourth: Flexible Servant-Related Forms over Centralized-Hierarchical Structures

Jesus shocked His disciples right out of their boots. He washed their feet (John 13:1–9, 14)! The boss never washed the feet of servants! What we see here is that the very nature of God is not one of power and control but loving and enabling service. And don't we take our cues from what God reveals concerning His very nature? Peter meant well, but he got it all wrong. And Jesus was quick to tell him. What he had witnessed was the essential nature of God's kingdom unfurled.

This principle of diverse forms of service dominated the structures of ministry in the first century. And what we see is that it is difficult, if not impossible, to discover a uniform structure of order and ministry. The major churches of Jerusalem, Antioch, Philippi, and Ephesus, from biblical perspectives, were really quite *diverse* in structure and worship but definitely *uniform* in unity of purpose and belief. (Worship was always centered around the breaking of the bread, but no universal form can be found in the first century.) However, unity of purpose is particularly noticeable regarding the desire to promote a universal mission of salvation.

An hierarchical church did not exist during the apostolic period, but a high regard for leadership most certainly did. Today, and indeed from about the very late part of the second century, the orders of bishops, priests, and deacons have become the norm. Indeed, in my own tradition, and in the *Canadian Book of Common Prayer*, a question is asked to those being prepared for confirmation:

> *Question.* What orders of ministers have been in the church from the apostles' time?

> *Answer.* Bishops, priests, and deacons.[13]

Wrong! Bishops, priests, and deacons did not exist as a threefold order of ministry in the first-century church.

---

13   *Book of Common Prayer*, 1962, 554.

Recently when I challenged a friend on the historical authenticity of this statement, he did not do it successfully—at least not from a historical or biblical perspective. But he did offer that there is an etymological connection between the words *episcopos* (bishop) and *hieros* (priest). He could not show me, from the Greek language, how this connection was there. *We concluded together* that the words had become connected solely by the way they had become associated in traditional practice.

The fact is, the word *priest* is never used in the New Testament to denote an order of Christian ministry. However, the word for priest (hieros) is used in three ways:

1. It is used to describe priests of the old order who continue to offer blood sacrifices.

2. It is used in Hebrews 7–9 to describe the eternal high priesthood of Jesus in making intercession for us all. As the writer strongly declares, the blood sacrifices of Aaron are now over forever. Jesus has offered Himself once and for all time.

3. The apostle Peter refers to the royal priesthood of all believers (1 Peter 2:9), and this priesthood is one of *proclamation* (Rev. 1:6).

Actually, a threefold order of ministry is mentioned in an old book of teaching called *The Didache*. (With possible additions, it may date back to approximately the year AD 100.) Here, "St. Clement's letter to the Corinthians, penned about AD 96, makes mention of 'bishops, presbyters, and deacons.'"[14]

About ten years later, a church leader in Antioch named Ignatius speaks of something close to this in the early second century. However, many historians agree that he was far ahead of what was to become the norm. "He was the first true advocate of the threefold ministry, although it was not for another fifty years or so that this kind of organization became universal."[15] However, I should mention that his

---

14   James A. Kleist, trans., *The Didache, Ancient Christian Writers.* (Pine Beach, NJ: Newman's Press, 1948), 7.

15   Ibid.

idea of a threefold ministry did not include a priesthood. The orders were bishops, elders, and deacons.

Actually, Ignatius (circa AD 107) seems to be the first to advocate a monarchical (ruling) position for one person to whom he entitles the exclusive word *bishop*. (At that time, Ignatius referred to a city bishop, not a diocesan prelate.) In other words, the bishop is the boss of the local church. He even suggests that it's the same thing as speaking to Christ when addressing *the bishop*.

If we accept that both Peter and Paul were martyred somewhere between AD 65 and 67, then it took *more than* thirty years after their deaths before there were even hints of a hierarchical order of ministry. Surely if an hierarchical structure had been an ecclesiastical necessity in the first-century church, then Jesus would have initiated it in His own time. Clearly, an evolution in that direction would certainly be contrary to the communal nature of the community He developed.

After seventy years of the church's entrance on to the stage of history, all twelve apostles had died, and there were still no signs of a hierarchical form of ministry. The twelve apostles had most certainly not set the stage for hierarchical forms. The directive of Paul to Titus (Titus 1:5) bears out the point. Does this mean the first-century church was inadequate? Does it mean that their principles were primitive? How arrogant it is to suggest that the success and superb diversity of the first-century church was borne upon primitive attitudes. (At least when compared to the supposed sophistication of a late second century that was moving toward becoming an institutionally focused hierarchy!)

Deacons, who had their origins in Jerusalem (Acts 6), do not appear in all the churches. For example, there were deacons in Jerusalem and Philippi, but there is clearly no mention of deacons in Antioch or Ephesus. A diaconate may have existed in these places, but there is no biblical proof of it (Acts 6:2–4, Phil. 1:1). We also note that, although there were seven deacons in Jerusalem, it was the apostles and elders who met to make the first theological decision amid serious dispute in Antioch. *Deacons didn't appear to be in the same room!* And at that time, it was prophets and teachers who made the decisions in Antioch (Acts 15:6, 13:1–3).

Certainly, in the Pauline churches, *there is a much clearer connection in the relationship of bishop to elder.* Kenneth Latourette, the historian, suggests, "Evidence seems to support the view that at the outset in some and perhaps all of the churches the designations of *elder* and *bishop* were used interchangeably for the same office."[16]

We may easily see this in all the Pauline churches. Almost all of the churches took their cue from the synagogues. There, the elders were the teaching and administrative people. But we see an instance where Paul (in Miletus) was unable to go north to Ephesus, so he asked their elders to meet him at Miletus. In Acts 20:17, he asked the *elders* to meet with him (vv. 18–27). Then he spoke of their past and his difficulties that were before him.

We note that Luke speaks of these leaders as *elders* (v. 28). Paul is here addressing those holding the office of elder. But he speaks of what *their function is*; what they do. He says that *they should act as overseers, shepherds, and guardians* of the faith. The Greek word that describes all of these functions is the same word: *episcopos.* That word is also used for *bishops.* And the same situation appears when Paul is describing to Timothy the qualifications for those elders who are called to do *episcopal* functions. (See 1 Tim. 3:1–7.) Also, when writing to Titus, his "partner in the gospel," he urges him to "appoint elders in every town" in Crete. And then he notes how the character of these *bishops* is exercised (Titus 1:5–7). (There is no evidence that Titus remained there to act as a ruling bishop over all those local churches.)

So much for the orders of bishops, priests, and deacons being essential to the good order of first-century Christian ministry!

Authority in the Church

The church in Antioch submitted the question of circumcision to the consideration of apostles and elders in Jerusalem. That fact alone shows that some sort of a network, and *some sense of mutual accountability,* had developed during New Testament days. After the destruction of

---

16   K. S. Latourette, *A History of Christianity,* vol. 1, revised edition. (New York: Harper and Row, 1975), 116.

Jerusalem, there was no place on earth, in the first-century church, that looked to a particular city as its focus. Such a flexible network was still required to ensure that the teaching of the apostles (which they had handed down to local church elders) was the paramount source of apostolic faith.

Although the nature of the church during the time of the apostles was *definitely not hierarchical*, nevertheless, the first-century church did call for the honoring of *godly leadership* (Heb. 13:17, 1 Pet. 5:1–5, 1 Tim. 3:1–3). The apostle Paul reluctantly wrote to the Corinthian church of his authority. But he did so humbly, reminding them of his weaknesses and his sacrifices. He also called for the honoring of those in leadership (1 Cor. 16:15–16, 2 Cor. 1:24, 8:23, 10:9–10, 12:11–12, 13:10).

It is clear that Jesus did not give ultimate authority to one person over all or even over the other apostles. That claim (made by some of Matt. 16:17–19, i.e., "and on this rock I will build my church") has become highly questionable to many scholars. To look at this verse in the context of consistency would mean that Jesus (in Matt. 28:19–20) is speaking of authority invested in Himself. Paul, most certainly did not afford Peter such a singular position of monarchical authority. Peter never asked for it (2 Cor. 11:5, 12:12) and it was never attributed to him, then. Actually, in a wonderful display of humility, Peter, in terms of theological ability, recognized Paul as one holding superior prowess. (2 Pet. 3:15–16). Paul certainly claimed equal authority (2 Cor. 12:11–12).

Nowhere in the four gospels do we see that any of the apostles recognize Peter as anything more than a spokesman for the group. Indeed, Paul refers to Jesus solely as *the Rock* (1 Cor. 10:4). As questionable as the Matthew verse may be, in terms of authenticity, we should note that in Mark 8 and Luke 9, when, in the same situation, Jesus asks the question, "Who do you say that I am?" there is no further comment made by Jesus. It is clearly the same situation (in Caesarea Philippi) as that in Matthew 16:13–20. Presuming the authenticity of source material, I noticed, when perusing three different Greek texts, that there was a consistency of the wording. Without exploring the Mathew verse in depth, I will simply note that, in the Greek, Jesus uses the word petros in more than one way. Petros is the masculine noun meaning rock. In the same verse, the second use of the noun sees the feminine use (petra). And that is in keeping with the feminine use of "my church-ecclesia." Clearly, Jesus is using the name of Peter to illustrate on what foundations the church of Christ will be built. Further exploration of Greek use, which I chose to leave out, seems to confirm this thesis.

Peter is one of the most wonderful and exciting characters in the entire Bible. I feel disturbed that, in general, Protestant people often do not give him the honor he deserves. Luke, the gospel writer, most certainly did. In the book of Acts, whatever praise he heaped upon Paul, he similarly honored Peter and vice versa. I believe Peter would be embarrassed to receive authority that was not equally afforded to his eleven apostolic brothers.

Such a thing as sole-monarchical authority (as Ignatius later tried to claim) is just *not in the nature of the Trinity.* God the Father is not the boss, but the focus of the Trinity of persons. His name symbolizes the ultimate *otherness of God.* Jesus gave His authority *to a community of apostles* while on the Mount of Ascension—eleven, to be precise (Matt. 28:18–20; Judas was not there)! So, is something missing here?

Similarly, we see the same nature of communal authority emerging in John's gospel. In one of His post-resurrection appearances, Jesus appeared to His apostles. But there really is something missing. Apostles! Thomas was not there (John 20:24), and neither had the replacement been made for Judas (Acts 1:21–26). What did those two apostles miss?

1. They had missed the apostolic commission to be sent into the world to bring peace (John 20:21).

2. They missed Christ's inbreathing of the Holy Spirit (v. 22).

3. They missed the authority to guard the way of reconciliation by forgiving or retaining sins (v. 23).

4. They missed the apostolic-communal authority to guard the faith, once delivered to them by Jesus.

Aren't all four points important? Yes, they are, but the *authority is in relation to the apostolic community* of those who had witnessed the resurrection and had been with Jesus for the entire length of His ministry (Acts 1:21–22). It was to that exclusive part of the community that gospel authority was granted. If there were ever a time when Jesus could have singled out anyone for individual authority, particularly over the other apostles, this would have been the time. But Jesus didn't. It is highly probable that the above four points did not relate to individual authority, particularly regarding monarchical authority.

But authority without power is meaningless.

We know that, at Pentecost, *power was given to the entire extended community of Jesus.* Therefore, in theological realities, it also extended to the new Eden community. (God breathed upon Adam and Eve, and that is precisely what Jesus did in this instance, Gen. 2:7, John 20:22.) It may be possible for some to assume that Thomas later received some sort of official recognition of all four of the above points. However, it is certainly not recorded. If, individually, it *was* a necessity, then surely John would have found space for one more line, at least. Matthias, the replacement for Judas (Acts 1:26), was not appointed until after the ascension of Jesus. And then there were ten!

What does this mean in terms of the passing down of individual authority? It doesn't mean anything! It means that the authority for the above four items was given to the apostolic community of the twelve alone! Thomas and Matthias didn't miss out on the authority at all. It was in the keeping of the apostolic community. Now this fits so much more easily into the nature of the Trinity, doesn't it?

Despite the adulations, royal courtesies, and authority attributed to popes, patriarchs, prelates, and priests, I believe the apostle Peter would never have allowed such exaltation be paid to himself by the rest of Jesus' community. (And indeed, they didn't give it!) As John the Baptist once said of Jesus, "He must increase, but I must decrease" (John 3:30). The Holy Spirit gave power and the graces to fulfill Christ's universal commission at Pentecost. But this power (as in the beginning) was given to an entire community of believers. Everything said or done had to be submitted to the authority of Christ's apostolic community and not to the opinion of one individual. In other words, *those in authority must also come under authority. Jesus transferred authority to the apostolic community rather* than investing selected individuals with monarchical power. We subscribe to the apostolic faith, not the faith of one apostle.

Leaders in authority may speak with authority but only in accord with the teaching of the entire historic community. That teaching goes back to the time of the apostles (Jude 3). For example, Jesus said to the ten, "If you forgive anyone his sins, they are forgiven; if you do not forgive them, they are not forgiven" (John 20:23). In other words, it is what the apostolic community of the twelve decided what is considered to be sin and what is not (e.g., what it is that separates God from His people). One of them could not determine that a particular act was not sin when the rest of the apostolic community decided it was. Subsequently, that apostolic consensus has been recorded in Scripture for the benefit of future generations.

If Jesus declared homosexual behavior (not a disposition in that direction) to be offensive to God's holiness, then one of the twelve would have no individual authority to decide otherwise. Incidentally, when this issue is held up to the light of creation theology (which is sadly lacking in these days), we can see that such behavior is sin. And Jesus certainly believed in creation theology and in God's original purposes for creation (Mark 10:6), and so did Paul (Rom.1:21–32). Unfortunately, in my own Canadian tradition, some individual bishops have decided that their own individual and institutional authority is all that is needed to declare that such behavior is not sin (Rom. 1:26–28, 32b, 1 Cor. 6:9–11). We can see that an individual person in authority *has no authority* when deciding contrary to that of the apostolic twelve.

I find it quite remarkable that the more liberal element in my own tradition appears to enjoy the hierarchical structures they have occupied. *Somehow, it all gets mixed up with power and control.* In North America, when some of these persons are elected to be bishops, they are beginning to demand that all the clergy should take oaths of allegiance to them individually. The fact is, in our Anglican ordination, we were all asked to submit to the authority of the bishop "and his successors." That means being under the authority of the historic apostolic community. *We do that once.* There's no need to repeat it for every new bishop. Certainly there is a need to come under authority for the maintenance of godly order in the community. But isn't that a far cry from being under the authority of an individual's personal opinion, particularly one who does not adhere to the whole apostolic faith?

Clearly the apostolic age witnessed a church thoroughly diverse in the ways it ordered its ministry. Wouldn't we expect this of our Trinitarian God? However, diversity may quite easily devolve to chaos. In other words, *diversity without common focus is chaos! But diversity focused under Christ's historically revealed authority is apostolic order!*

I am not questioning here why an hierarchy was allowed to develop in the church. If diversity made allowance for this at that time, then why should not godly diversity also abolish it? Isn't eighteen hundred years enough for that little experiment to prove its kingdom worth or not?

Fifth: Gifting of the Entire Priesthood of Believers

> But you are a chosen people, a royal priesthood, a holy nation, a people belonging to God, that you may declare the praises of him who called you out of darkness into his wonderful light. Once you were not a people, but now you are the people of God. (1 Pet. 2:9–10)

Where, in the entire New Testament, can you find the term *the priest* of the local church? Or put in more Protestant terms, where can you find *the pastor* of the local church? You can't! Irenaeus, as far back as the late second century, equated positions of ministry with spiritual gifting.

Clearly, in the first-century church we see the dominance of charismatic gifting over institutional titles. Offices held in the church did not relate to institutional position but tended to be consistent with spiritual gifting.[17] Ignatius was certainly a prophet-bishop.[18] A little later, Irenaeus (c. AD 180) speaks of gifts in the Church that include casting out demons, knowledge, visions, prophecy, healing, and raising

---

17   Ronald A. N. Kydd, *Charismatic Gifts in The Early Church.* (Peabody, MA: Hendrickson Publishers, 1984), 9.

18   Ibid., 17.

the dead.[19] He also wrote of people who "through the Spirit do speak all kinds of languages and bring to light, for the general benefit the hidden things of men and declare the mystery of God."[20]

Then What about Laypersons?

In the first-century church (i.e., in and beyond New-Testament times), there was no such thing as a layperson! There were just people who were graced with spiritual gifts.

> The word *laikos-* 'belonging to the common people' …
> was first used to describe Christians by Clement of
> Rome at the end of the first century. He used 'layman'
> (*laikos*) in his epistle to the Corinthians to describe the
> place of laity in worship when the presbyters were being
> deprived of their functions.[21]

Paul Stevens continues, "One searches the New Testament in vain for a theology of the laity. Neither layman nor priests can be found in it."[22])

Indeed, I noticed, when trying to trace the use of the word *laos* in terms of ministry function that it is used only in the Old Testament. (I am referring to the Greek Septuagint.) For example, when King Josiah gave instructions for the restoration of the Passover (621 BC), he used the word twice (2 Chron.35:5, 7). Here, he is contrasting the activity of the priestly class of the Levitical tribe with the common people.

So-Called Laypersons Did It

There were some marvelous ministries that occurred through so-called laypersons in New Testament days. Phillip, who was a deacon of Jerusalem, performed signs and wonders while preaching in Samaria (Acts 8:4–7,

---

19   Ibid., 44.

20   George Williams and Edith Waldvogel, *The Charismatic Movement.* (Grand Rapids, MI: William B. Eerdmans, 1975), 66.

21   Paul R. Stevens, "On the Abolition of the Laity," *Crux Magazine*, June 1995/Vol. XXX1, no. 2, 5.

22   Ibid., 6.

13). He had four daughters who exercised the gift of prophecy in their local church (Acts 21:9). Note: as a deacon, Philip baptized (Acts 8:13, 38). What about Ananias? He's one of my heroes. Where would the entire Christian church be if it were not for the obedience of this so-called layman? Certainly Ananias didn't want anything to do with the apostle Paul, who at that time was called Saul. Saul was the cause for Christians being killed all over the place!

Scared as he was:

1. Ananias laid hands on Saul.

2. Saul was healed of blindness.

3. Then Saul received the gift of the Holy Spirit.

It was the anointing for a magnificent ministry to the Gentiles. Little did Ananias know that through his obedience, Paul's writings would help feed the church for more than two thousand years in the future.

Isn't it strange that Ananias gets very little recognition from the historic orthodox churches of today? Why is that? Probably because *in later years*, it was thought he did something supposedly reserved for professional clergy! To those who claim that apostolic order has always come down through apostolic laying on of hands, they have a hard time in proving it. God used a so-called layman to launch the ministry of a truly outstanding apostle—whether we like it or not! I believe there is a church named after Ananias in Damascus, but you will look very hard to find formal recognition of him in most orthodox claimants to *apostolic succession*.

In terms of church organization, Kenneth Latourette sums up the situation in this way: "In any event, the latter part of the first century and the fore part of the second century still saw variety in the forms of organization of the churches."[23] In other words, forms and orders of ministry until the end of the first century were flexible, yet they did maintain what I have described as *essential principles of apostolicity*.

---

23   Latourette, *A History of Christianity*, 118.

An illustration of the relation of gifts to ministries

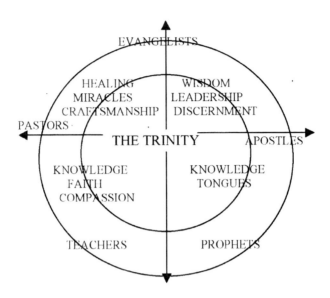

What we see here is an order as Paul described it to the Ephesian church. Maybe the church in Antioch operated in a slightly different way (Acts 13:1–2). Here, the leadership (*archoi*) seems to be composed of prophets and teachers. We must remember that *authority* for the safeguarding of the apostolic faith is in the keeping of the apostles, including people like Paul and Barnabas. The *power* for kingdom ministry belongs to the entire people of God (Acts 2:1–4).

To repeat, when the apostle Paul declared his credentials to the Corinthian church, he noted the following:

> For I am not in the least inferior to the 'super-apostles,' even though I am nothing. The things that mark an apostle—signs, wonders and miracles—were done among you with great perseverance. (2 Cor. 12:11–12)

> So Paul and Barnabas spent considerable time there, speaking boldly for the Lord, who confirmed the message of his grace by enabling them to do miraculous signs and wonders. (Acts 14:3)

I wonder, if such works of the Spirit were requirements today regarding apostolic leadership in the church, how many bishops or other leaders would not qualify where many so-called lay people do? I think of someone like Heidi Baker and her husband, Rolland. They have a wonderfully anointed ministry to the poor and the sick in Mozambique. Signs and wonders occur with regularity in that ministry. They wonder why they see so little of them when they return to North America. Her book, *Expecting Miracles*, may provide an answer.[24]

On the other hand, similar experiences regularly happen when Andrew White (known as the vicar of Baghdad) ministers salvation and healing to mostly Muslim people in that Islamic country. In a very refined British accent, he also questions why signs and wonders lessen when he returns to England. Surely they represent what it means for the Spirit to minister through the entire body of Christ. In this case, institutional titles count for little. Indeed, both testify to the fact that disciples, whom they have taught, regularly see the growth of the church occurring through signs and wonders.

I have mentioned those five apostolic principles for two reasons: *First, they are all perfectly applicable and absolutely vital for ministry in the twenty-first century. Second, I believe with all my heart that the group-based church provides an excellent or even the very best vehicle through which the expression of all these principles may be conveyed.*

I do find it necessary to repeat what I have already mentioned. Clearly I am not referring to the average church that encourages people to go into home groups. Most of these churches are program churches that incorporate home groups into their process. I am speaking of group-based churches. *The group-based church is the process!* This structure, and its enormous potential, will become clearer a little later.

---

24   Heidi Baker and Rolland Baker, *Expecting Miracles*. (Grand Rapids, MI: Chosen Books, 2007), 37–40.

CHAPTER 7

Changing World, Unchanging Gospel

*W*hat an indescribable difference there is in ministering for God in today's world, at least compared to the world in which I was ordained! One thing is certain: the world is changing, fast. Apparently in the world we now double our knowledge at least once every year. I can't even keep up with the varieties of boot polish! The question is, how do we minister in today's rapidly changing world? We have one certainty in the middle of a field of uncertainty: *The gospel of Jesus never changes but its methodology must.*

That's why Verna and I didn't think we were crazy in searching for a church that applies first-century apostolic principles to our twenty-first-century world. Will we ever find one? I doubt it. But if the world keeps changing, where do we get off? Some sociologists tell us that the culture of the West changes about every nineteen to twenty years. That's not hard to accept. Just take church connections, for example.

Twenty-five years ago, you could stop a stranger in the street and ask him, "What church do you stay away from?" Most likely, he would tell you. Probably he would also admit that he wasn't a regular attendee but at best a CE member of a mainline church (CE means Christmas and Easter)! Nearly everyone headed for a candlelight, silent night Christmas Eve. As a pastor, it was hard not to welcome everyone with the words, "Nice to see you again!" And at the end of the service, "See you next year!"

That day is long past. The church can no longer expect the world to take notice of anything it says. Why should it? Most mainline churches have worked very hard to establish themselves as chaplains to the culture anyway. "Ask us what to bless next, and we will do it," we say, especially in mainline churches. The result is that there is little discernible difference between the values and goals of the world and those of the church. Why should the world take the slightest bit of notice to anything the church says? The world can say those same things and without a religious gloss. In other words, *the western mainline church has lost its prophetic voice to the world. No longer does it present a position that is counter-culture. The weary old Hebrew prophets are dead, and so are those of a post-modern and mildewed Christendom.*

Then why are Christians counter-culture in thought and behavior? Can we be counter-culture and still love our neighbors? The reason is because our lives, our hopes, our goals, and our values are set on the kingdom of God first and foremost (Matt. 6:33). We come alongside people with our kingdom values—not in judgment but to demonstrate what God intended for His kingdom in Eden. In that way, the church continually needs a prophetic voice to remind us of how we demonstrate kingdom life to the world.

1. It seems to me that what is most needed in the entire Christian church are churches that will risk becoming *meta churches*. The Greek word *meta* means change. Carl George puts it this way:

    The word *Meta-Church* doesn't describe a church form so much as it announces the fact that 'doing church' in our current way is an inadequate vehicle for all that Christ has called his body to do and be. We must change our thinking, our imagination of what God is trying to do. We must attune our hearts and methods to how he will go about doing it … Every church on earth with greater than twenty thousand in attendance uses some variation of a technology we analyze as Meta-Church. For example, here are some observations …

The world's largest church—*more than a dozen times larger than any other in the history of Christendom*—is cell based. It happens to belong to the Assemblies of God family of churches, but the two largest Presbyterian, the two largest Methodist, and the largest Baptist church in the world are, likewise, cell-driven churches.

Australia: A church in Brisbane has about four thousand members in three hundred cells. In Sydney, a cell movement begun in the mid-1970s now blankets the entire western side of that city.

Portugal: This country, where Protestants comprise only 1 percent of the population, is the birthplace of a cell church that now encompasses some thirty thousand people.

Chile: The largest church on the continent of South America, located in Santiago, is cell based and convenes at least fifty thousand people for corporate worship each week.

Ivory Coast: A church in Abidjan, planted in 1975, now has thirty thousand members and more than two thousand cell groups.

Malaysia: A church in Singapore has burgeoned from an attendance of two hundred in 1968 to well over five thousand at present, with more than four hundred cell groups.[25]

---

25   Carl F. George, *The Coming Church Revolution*. (Grand Rapids, MI: H. Revell, 1994), 31–34.

Of course, here in this book, I am using the word *meta* as demonstrated in one particular way because I am biased. I believe the group-based church has far more opportunity to adopt a meta mind-set than any other church form.

The Old Has Passed Away?

More and more, contemporary scientists are awestruck by their ever-growing and exponential questions. A much higher percentage of them are now looking to God as the Creator and the one who gives purpose to life. The fact is, although the world is constantly changing, there are remarkable parallels of pluralistic values in which the first-century church lived. We didn't invent pluralism in our generation! We remember that during the time of the apostles, Christians and Jews were accused of being atheists, and that's because they were monotheists. They believed in one God. (That was a very strange thing in a polytheistic world.) The extraordinary *power of the gospel of the living Christ is clearly the only news for every age, culture, and time.*

I would like us to examine the question of whether the unchanging gospel is relevant for our time. (I get bored with that word. Relevance is a word so badly used in connection with witnessing to a contemporary world.) The unchanging gospel of Jesus Christ is astonishingly pertinent for today. But the way the church presents its gospel must always undergo a scrutiny that is open to change. There seems to be a universal cry among older people in church congregations: "Where are the young people?"

Despairingly, the same tired people vainly hope, "The young people will do it." Who will keep the institution going? The fact is that *the young people are just not interested—at least not in a self-aggrandizing and institutional focus!* For most of them, the churches have ceased to be in touch with a post-modern, techno-communication age. These young people are also a very busy and stressed. But there is yet another factor here: *This generation is not a people of memory!*

It's not a new situation. The ancient Hebrews experienced this problem about thirty-two hundred years ago! In just one generation, a people of common memory had lost it!

> After that whole generation had been gathered to their
> fathers, another generation grew up, who knew neither
> the Lord nor what he had done for Israel. (Judges 2:10)

Isn't it amazing what can happen when it's just churchy culture
and tradition that's passed down and not the power to sign historical
principles and purposes of the gospel? Jesus faced the problem a lot. The
result in ancient Israel was:

> In those days Israel had no king; everyone did as he saw
> fit. (Judges 21:25)

That's precisely the position we are in today! In one generation,
much of the mainline churches, in their desire to accommodate the
culture, have become indistinguishable from it (except the church adds
a dab of spirituality)! Consequently, the children of those who had the
faith passed on to them, and who inherited church forms, cultures and
historical edifices of worship, have mostly grown up as a generation
without a memory! Not surprisingly, few people have a common memory
of church, its purpose, its values, or its contributions to the social needs
of the local community. In the embryonic days of Israel, it was not a
question of the Hebrew community versus the world but of Israel's
purpose in the world. It seems to be the apostolic purpose of Genesis
12:1–3 that has been lost. Apart from that primary purpose, what did
the traditions mean?

*As in the first century, the church now treads on virgin territory for the
gospel of Jesus Christ. Christendom is dead. Therefore, no longer may we
expect easy passage into the avenues of our culture.*

Spirituality versus Truth

It's not the job of the church to offer dabs of spirituality to a bored and
ever-changing culture. We are called to offer Jesus as the Truth, and that
has to be done knowing the risk involved. Indeed, the gospel itself may be
assaulted for its blatant counter-cultural nature. But that doesn't mean
to say the gospel is offered in a repulsive and arrogant way. (Actually, the
church's primary purpose is not to change culture but to demonstrate

the much-superior way of God's kingdom. Culture tends to be reshaped when the church effectively witnesses to the power of God at work.) *We remember that the gospel is essentially relational because our God is relational in His Trinitarian nature.*

Although Christians may become more and more disenchanted with modern culture, we must also give credit where it is due. There are many good and desirable characteristics emerging in the children of this generation. In this post-modern age, when Generation X and Y people are sometimes throwing off the acquisitive, materialistic goals of their parents, there is a search for something more. Nevertheless, our son Mark (a Gen-X pastor) tells us that his three Gen-Y daughters are certainly in the age of the entitlement culture. That is a culture believing they are entitled to whatever their little hearts desire. And they deserve it now!

Who are these Gen-X and Gen-Y people? They are the young adults who were born between 1965 and 1983, with few exceptions. Colleen Carroll singles out a growing minority of potential leaders (from orthodox backgrounds) who challenge today's contemporary pluralistic and postmodern trends.[26]

She identifies the majority of that generation as those who "reject or undermine universal standards and absolute-truth claims, and all celebrate the leveling of hierarchies and the equalizing or blending of diverse ideologies."[27] Indeed, the young orthodox believers "resist any compromise of the essential tenets of orthodoxy as capitulation to secular culture."[28] Interestingly, these new leaders are also people who yearn for mystery.[29] With an educated guess on the directions in which the world is moving, let's ask this question: *If you wanted to have a one-world order, how would you go about it?*

That isn't as stupid a question as it may sound. I think there are a number of reasons why some people would like that sort of world.

---

26   Colleen Carroll, *The New Faithful.* (Chicago: Loyola Press, 2002), 13–14.

27   Ibid., 15.

28   Ibid., 16.

29   Ibid., 15.

The first one might be a *religious* one. Imagine the whole world being dominated by one religion? Children would not be taught in the home but the classroom. The second might be a *financial* one. Imagine what it would be like if there were no barriers to trading your goods anywhere in the world. Or imagine if there were no *power motives* that caused wars between acquisitive nations. Religion, finances, and huge egos (like Adolph Hitler's) have been at the root of untold death and suffering. For some, the Bible actually predicts that a one-world order will emerge; it will occur during latter days (Rev.13:1-8) We have never been in an age where that could be possible—until now! *And we can't assume that the past ways in which the church witnessed to the truth of the gospel will always be effective in today's world.* I'll take a very, very brief look into some possible indicators because *the new truth is now called political correctness.*

Religion

The Western world (with its highly industrialized bases) has been built around Judeo-Christian values. That hasn't been much of a problem in the past. Indeed, it's been a great help in the very long agricultural era. It was also useful in the industrial era. Don't steal, keep your family together, don't covet, be loyal, and uphold the truth uniting the country in freedom, don't bonk someone on the head and he won't bonk you, etc. But that doesn't work in an easily accessible techno-communication world. One simple example: If commercial media isn't successful in creating covetousness, it's out of business! The tenth commandment and the Sermon on the Mount go flying out of the window! (After all, these are both standards of the kingdom of God.)

We may also wonder, in this speedily texting world, how, with an ever-diminishing vocabulary, young people can grasp the transcendental vistas that required words that grasped for a sense of otherness. We may not meet young people at that place, but if we are to be effective as disciple-makers, we cannot leave them where they are. Incidentally, that is one of the problems with seeker-sensitive churches. People longing for maturity are constantly tired of clichés that fail to raise them to a higher level of transcendence.

Change was frowned on in the past, *but it's necessary now.* Both loyalty and the idea of deciding to remain in one location won't work today if you want to live up to a certain lifestyle or *your entitlement*. And that's true, even if it means breaking up the foundation of your culture. I'm speaking about the family. In those older times, the family was foundational to learning and living values. But those days are no longer with us. In this techno-age, it's the children who inform parents about this ever-changing world. Should we be surprised that our new value system could not arrive until we experienced a serious breakdown of the family? How did that happen? How were we prepared for that? What we somewhat naturally accept today is quite the opposite of the communal values once learned at home. We are used to hearing: "After all, you can do anything. And you should because you're worth it."

Immigration is very important in this globalized world. The labor market is vital. What about people arriving in the West and bringing with them all of their Eastern beliefs and values? It could, and does, lead to cultural conflict. So what's the answer? Simple! *There is no absolute truth!* But *spirituality* is fine. Spirituality is personal, it's individual, and it doesn't have to affect anyone else. What you believe is not intended to affect society. It's an individual thing; it's good for you. There goes John 14:6 right out of the window! Every religion is right (even if they are contradictory). And if you don't accept that, then *you are very intolerant and bigoted*. In this world, who wants to be thought of in those terms?

Tolerance, not the Truth, becomes the way of the enlightened. Tell an insecure, middle-aged, middle-class guy that he's intolerant, and he'll become whatever you want him to be! *Truth can be divisive, but a me-centered spirituality is harmless.* My truth is not your truth, but as long as we can both be spiritual, we'll get along really well. It's spirituality and relativism that make the new world tick. Never before in the entire history of civilization has there been a means of communication that can brainwash a globally minded community into new ways of thinking, and our present communication media is a powerful ally in this process.

Jesus cannot be compared with any other religious leader in the entire history of the world. Not only was He the finest person who ever lived (that may be a relative statement), but He is also God (that is an absolute statement, unless He is a liar, John 5:18). My book *Time and* the *Biblical Bang* may be helpful here. The truth is Jesus is both God and Man (2 Cor. 5:19), but that would be politically incorrect, even if it is the truth! What an absurd world we live in! Are we being prepared for what is to come?

Financial

Right now, the European community is looking again at the Euro currency. Is it best for the community to keep one form of barter? The European financial difficulties possibly could be resolved if there was only one global form of barter. Imagine: no country could peg the value of their own dollar or ruble. But it would have to be controlled by an empowered United Nations, of course. Does 666 begin to look more sinister (Rev. 3:18)? We expected those predictions more from doomsday Bible-thumpers than white-collar young visionaries. Those Bible-thumpers were easy to recognize. They were people holding a Bible in one hand and a daily newspaper in the other.

What if the contents of all the newspapers were to be controlled in that new world order? (Believe it or not, that even happened to me in my own now-secularized church denomination. My articles for its national newspaper began to be censored. I refused to allow further publication.) Who would be able to barter with the 666 (Rev. 13:16–17)? Would it not be those who willingly conform to the values and demands of a world government? It is now possible to have a strip inserted in the forehead that, when scanned, would allow you to purchase anything. It could also reveal everything about you, including your bank accounts. What if your values mean you don't qualify for that little strip?

All of this used to sound bizarre. It emanated from the minds of fanatics. In many ways, I agree with that observation. But the problem is that the technicalities are available *right now*! It's just the *chaotic desperation* that's needed for further implementation. When that appears and the despair is growing stronger, the time for a global and social reorganization will emerge. Citizens of the world will lose the charm and pleasure of the diversities and freedom we now take for granted. The techno-universal language of political correctness will overcome the barriers of Babel.

Power-Seeking Egoism

The philosophic superman of Nietzsche's utopia only needs desperation and despair to facilitate its false promise of hope. Hitler, a fan of Nietzsche, thought he or his country could be the superman to achieve it. Both of them are dead now. But the idea certainly lingers on in the minds of power-hungry people. In a globalized community, the idea of a superman residing in an individual appears to be obscure. But superman, or the beast of Revelation 13:16–18, could easily become a system. Its adherents would be a faithful and politically correct people. As in the garden of Eden, Satan appeals to the human ego and tells us that we cannot possibly die; we are immortal!

Does God Have an Alternative?

Yes, He does! After all, He is the Lord of time. But it all has to do with His kingdom. He had it all thought out before time began (1 Pet. 1:20, Rev. 13:7–8). And it is in this world, running toward a chaotic end, that signs of God's kingdom are appearing. The outward focus expressed in evangelism is a major sign of hope. It is God's hope, not through a degenerating earth but through Christ's body, the church. (This is one reason why commitment to the body of Christ is the third plank in the process of my *Growing in Christ* seminar.)

There really are major changes in this present age. Even more, science and philosophy are operating hand in glove. During the days of the Enlightenment (eighteenth-century Europe), it was philosophy that tended to follow the predictable rules of Newtonian science. In other words, "If I can't see it, then it doesn't exist," or "Give me undisputable facts."

Things are different now. Modern scientists would laugh at that statement. Every time scientists think they are near to solving a major question, they discover they have just opened up a Pandora's Box full of new questions. Instead of hearing, "One day science will give us the answer," now we are more likely to hear, "We will never arrive at the answers to all our questions."

In this postmodern age, *scientists tend to replace clergy as the modern priests of mystery.* "Physicists are now as much scientists of the invisible as theologians used to be."[30] This generation tends to bypass the limitations of a worldview that's rooted in the rationalism of the Enlightenment. As one modern astrophysicist tells us, the modern physicist is now more likely to debate questions about God than ever in the last hundred years, and "Astronomers who do not draw theistic or deistic conclusions are becoming rare."[31] This unabashed search for mystery causes people of all types, occupations, and intellectual achievements to move in exciting and often *contradictory and bizarre directions.*

The main reason for these apparent contradictions is that *absolute truth* seems to be a low priority for most people. It may as well be a stale cheese sandwich. Maybe some of it has to do with the awesome interest in the world of microphysics. For example, around 1926, Werner Heisenberg spoke of a theory that he called the Uncertainty Principle. Without elaborating on it, Heisenberg would say (from the perspective of the behavior of micro-particles) the reality of a particle's behavior is dependent upon the observer. Now physicists have found the so-called God particle—an elusive part of the atom that may unlock questions of the relationships within the atom.

Philosophers asked questions in a similar way. "Did a tree fall in a forest if nobody heard it?" All of this may have contributed to the older philosophy of John Paul Sartre. It was called Existentialism. Here the experience of the *I or me* becomes the center of reality. In other words, truth becomes relative to every person.

No one wants a stale cheese sandwich, so truth is no longer the goal it was in the past. (It is to modern science but not in popular thinking). The problem with that idea is that both macro (big) and micro (small) physics are needed for this modern, techno-communication age. Both were needed to put Neil Armstrong on the moon! In popular thought, the strange paradox persists that truth is still relative to me. When it comes to the real questions, our present *attitudes* can get in the way of truth.

---

30   Leonard I. Sweet, *Quantum Spirituality*. (Dayton, OH: Venture Ministries, 1994), 5.

31   Hugh Ross, *The Creator and the Cosmos*. (Colorado Springs, CO: NavPress, 2001), 32.

Getting behind the superficiality of "what is good for me," those questions are coming back. "If there is a Creator-God, then He must have had a purpose. Maybe God actually has a purpose for my life. What is it?" Now you would think a person with brains occupying the cavity in his head would not be satisfied with anything but the truth, but "It ain't necessarily so." Why not?

Well, a lot of people don't know it, but they have a spirit inside of them that wants to relate to its source; that is, to God (Gen. 1:27, 2:7)! It doesn't matter where in the world you go, people are trying to satisfy this spiritual longing inside of them. Not surprisingly, there are many of those religions that are based in nature, so they are not really helpful because, in our human feebleness, we need help and revelation from above. It's called salvation. Now wouldn't you think this hunger in us would cause everybody to look for truth, no matter where it leads? Jesus thought that way:

> And you will know the truth, and the truth will make
> you free." (John 8:32)

It really wasn't very long ago when eggheads in a coffee bar would slobber over the question, "What is truth?" That's the same question Pontius Pilate asked Jesus (John 18:38). Of course, he expected Jesus to engage in a bout of Platonic philosophy. Jesus was silent. If Pilate couldn't see the truth in front of him, what was the point?

Like the stale cheese sandwich, truth has gone out of the window. But why? It's because very few people ask the right questions anymore. "Your truth is fine for you, and mine is good for me." That's the way people think today—not because it's the correct way but because questions of absolute truth are not worth the price of a coffee anymore. If truth is not a goal in our contemporary world, what replaces the hunger? It's spirituality! As long as we are *spiritual*, that will get us a free coffee in any company.

We can see, then, that spirituality and truth are not always the same thing. But spirituality makes us feel good. *And that's the religion of our age.* Paradoxically, there seems to be a slight resurgence of younger people attending some churches today. And we had thought they had gone forever. Nevertheless, to put this in perspective, in the United States, "There are 31 percent fewer young people who are regular churchgoers than in the heat of the cultural revolution of the 1970s."[32] The problem is that much leadership of the church thinks these new pew-fillers are there in a search of truth. Most of the younger people are there because *it satisfies a spirituality; it satisfies a growing sense of mystery.* They will shop around until they hear profound words or even experience cozy feelings. They are monosyllabic words; it is often King James language, Starbuck talk, renaissance music, rock music, ancient hymns, or songs with "I" on every other line.

We are in a very spiritual generation. And when the church panders to spirituality before the Truth, we pave a pathway to hell on soft cushions. A person is the truth, and He is Jesus (John 14:6; Matt.11:27)! Jesus is not a philosophy; He is the truth in flesh and blood!

Well, that is what the church has always believed, even if it meant persecution. And there is sure a lot of that today. Without Jesus as the very heart of all life-giving activity, the church exists simply to offer its many varieties of spirituality. As we will see, the first-century church was truly a meta community. In Liddell and Scott's Greek-English Lexicon (2001) the word, *meta*, speaks of change of place, condition, plan. So the word is often used to speak of an ability to change one's way of thinking or doing. Of course, in biblical days, they didn't change the message of the gospel, but depending on where they were, they would deliver it in ways that were understood in the culture. In other words, in praxis (what we do), it was a *diverse* church. There is hope for a remnant within this generation. Gabe Lyons describes this remnant as *The Next Christians*:

> The six characteristics that set apart the
> next Christians are that they are,
> Provoked, not offended
> Creators, not critics
> Called, not employed

---

32   Gabe Lyons, *The Next Christians.* (New York: Doubleday, 2010), 23.

Grounded, not distracted
In community, not alone
Countercultural, not "relevant.[33]

It is a generation more concerned with *who you are* than *what you do*. They are more interested in how effective you are than the title you carry around. That idea doesn't easily appear to have penetrated the Christian world of historic orthodoxy yet. But the servant-minded Jesus demonstrated it throughout His entire ministry. So the next Christians say, "Show me what you do; don't tell me your status."

Consequently, in relational ways and with industrial ease, they connect scientific and religious disciplines. In their desire to operate in networking ways to achieve their goals, they are becoming less and *less interested in hierarchical systems*. But that doesn't mean they have thrown out the baby with the bathwater. As far back as 1970, Alvin Toffler predicted the demise of hierarchical structures in business life and called for the adoption of *sideways approaches*.[34]

A younger churchgoing generation will not attend church where they will be met with judgment. Nor will they attend where *the old people* expect them to take over institutional duties. But they do delight in being in situations where lives are being changed in positive ways. They are not good financial givers but desire to see their money being spent on people, not on old systems.

The apostle Paul was a man of genuine humility. Not threatened by differences, he accepted people without imposing judgment on them. His discourse on Mars Hill is a perfect example of a man who had the genius to meet people at the level of natural religion and take them to heights of transcendence. (See Acts 17.)

Verna and I saw a wonderful example of this when we opened our home in Victoria to ex-convicts, street people, and church people who were looking for more. We had retired from our church work in

33   Ibid., 67.

34   Alvin Toffler, *Future Shock*. (New York: Random House, 1984),123, 126.

Metchosin (Victoria, Canada) and had begun a house church in our own home. I was amazed at the amount of respect exhibited there.

One thing I noticed about the street kids was very revealing. They displayed an enormous amount of respect for me but only because I had equally respected them. One day, I asked the group of about twenty-five or thirty, "How would you feel if a couple of homosexual guys came here next week?" Without exception, all of them eagerly said they would look forward to it. Those two years were most certainly a highlight of my professional church experience. Much of what I learned during those two years inspired me to view the institution of the church through the filters of the kingdom of God. *For much of my professional life, inadvertently, I viewed the kingdom of God through the filters of the church institution.* Jesus told us to seek the kingdom first (Matt. 6:33). In putting this perspective first in all things, I began to envision a method of bringing together a fellowship of home group–based churches.

Surely as people search for deeper meaning in life, they expect to see it expressed in relationships. Isn't this precisely where the church can be at its best? The Lord is leading His Church into new ways of coming alongside the world He loves (John 3:16).

CHAPTER 8

Worship and First-Century Practice

"The chief end of man is to glorify God and to enjoy Him, forever."

These are the paraphrased words of St. Augustine and are often recited from the Presbyterian, Scottish Catechism. It's really all about *presence.* On our many visits to churches, Verna and I asked the questions, "Did we get caught up in the presence of God today? Would we look forward to coming back next Sunday?" Was it too much to expect that the experience of real presence would propel us back there next Sunday?

Actually, over the course of that year and a half, broadly speaking, we came alongside two types of church organizations. The first group was what I will call Protestant-Evangelical. They were churches such as Baptist, Alliance, Pentecostal, Presbyterian, and other mainline affiliations. Included with them were the more Independent Evangelical churches. We may say they evolved from sixteenth-century reaction to the Roman Church. I might easily include the recent Vineyard churches here. The second group was the churches that retained some earlier historical form and structure. It also included churches of post-Reformation persuasion. Lumped together, they were churches, such as Anglican (Episcopal), Lutheran, Roman Catholic, etc.

Throughout the first group, the liturgy mostly took almost exactly the same form: a lot of singing followed by a lot of preaching, and then everyone went home. The congregation sang, they listened, and they gave money. Sometimes announcements were thrown in somewhere, but often they were on the big screen and were read before the singing. Rarely did we ever encounter any period that may be described as *entering into the mystery* or moving in a process direction. In the larger churches, music was often offered in a very professional manner. It was often done very well but could easily slip into a performance mode. (But this could also occur with a large and sophisticated choir of either group.)

Almost everywhere there was really *little room allowed for the spontaneous or informal movement of the Spirit.* In the larger churches, the allotted time for the service was held quite rigidly. An earlier or later service often determined a very strict time pattern for each service. *It was too much to expect that the Holy Spirit could lead into spontaneous silence, revelations, or empowered ministries.*

What about the second type? Almost without exception, these churches honored some form in the procession of the worship. At least, it was orderly, even if it was in a different way than the apostle Paul suggested (1 Cor. 14:40). Clearly, with Jewish backgrounds, the apostles were used to some liturgical form of worship. Obviously, as we see in the Gentile context of Corinth (and in churches to the middle of the second century), form plus informality became the norm. Of course, most churches of the second group were offering a variety of reformed liturgies. Some dated their forms right back to the time of the sixteenth century and much beyond that. *The careful choosing of theologically precise words at least pointed to some sense of otherness and transcendence.* A liturgical pattern at least guaranteed a forward movement of form through essential elements of worship. Every, or almost every, word was recited from the appropriate book of prayer. Significantly, the congregation usually responded with appropriate and set words.

Remarkably, the very same thing happened in the services of type one or type two. There was little or no room allowed for the Holy Spirit to move in directions of His choosing. *Both types were petrified by silence,* so if there were to be any personal ministry, it would never be as the Spirit revealed it, there and then. Quite honestly, that sort of revelation very rarely occurred. But, in some churches, ministry was reserved after the service and to those who came forward to the ministry team. (Thank God for those faithful teams.) Although I spent considerable time helping out at a type-one church, if I have to compromise what I am looking for, I would rather settle for a type-two church because in those kinds of churches, *that sense of the otherness of God is easier to find.* Otherness and imminence are both necessary factors in worship. However, when the service is conducted in a monotone voice and the worshippers have allowed the flattened and passionless words to float over them, we found the service could easily become boring without some considerable effort.

Both types, although they might claim to be biblical and traditional, were not biblical or traditional enough!

Indeed, it may not be unkind to observe that, if the Twelve Apostles were to appear, suddenly, they may not recognize most of these worship services to be that of a first-century church!

We are not at all certain of the variety of worship forms in the first-century church. Although Paul spent some time with Peter (Gal. 1:18), we don't have reason to believe that the Pauline churches worshipped in exactly the same way as did those in Jerusalem or other places. However, according to scriptural hints (e.g., Eph. 5:19–20), it is difficult to imagine that first-century churches suppressed the leading of the Spirit. Maybe we could therefore heed Paul in a general way. Here is a comment written to the Corinthian church:

> When you come together, each one has a hymn, a lesson,
> a revelation, a tongue, or an interpretation. Let all things
> be done for building up. (1 Cor. 14:26)

Clearly, the entire congregation is here invited to be participants in the form and in the spiritual gifts used in the service. That leading of the Spirit mostly occurred at the time of the worship in "spiritual songs." (Eph.5:19) Possibly some preparation had been made, particularly regarding the ministry of the Word. In almost all of those services we attended, the admonition of Paul that, "all things should be done decently and in order" was absolutely no problem. It was no problem because rarely was anything of an informal nature risked! Few of those above elements were ever allowed to happen! (I wonder how many of those churches promoted the *Alpha* program. Of course, most had not heard of my own *Growing in Christ* course!) At least that process of basic discipleship encourages ways and means by which participants may be open to the Spirit's leading in worship and in other ways.

What Is Liturgy?

It's not a dirty word. And if understood properly (as in the first century), it could easily be adapted for type-one or type-two churches. The word *liturgy* is actually derived from two Greek words: *lithos* (stone) and *ergos* (work). The word speaks of building worship, like building a stone structure. But the building is about worship. And it's not done by one person but *by all the participants. Liturgy was always the worship of the people; they were not spectators!* It is probably a surprise to some, but the twelve apostles really did worship with some liturgical form.

For example, the breaking of the bread (1 Cor. 11:23–34) was couched in familiar words of the Passover, and those of the cup of fellowship and of blessing. Such words were also employed in the Kiddush meal. (It was a fellowship celebration of a rabbi with his disciples.) While the apostles remained in Jerusalem, they attended worship at the temple (Acts 2:46), and they also broke bread in homes and when they all met together. Peter and John regularly attended afternoon worship at the temple. (It was preparation for working life of the next day, Acts. 3:1)

On his missionary journeys, the apostle Paul initially met with other Jews during the worship of the synagogue (Acts 13:5; there are lots of these examples in the book of Acts, even after Paul said he wouldn't go to the Jews). The point that I want to make is that, very quickly, the church at large amalgamated the Jewish worship of the temple and synagogue. Temple worship emphasized the sacrifice of Christ, and that of the worshippers (Rom. 12:1). *It was the temple and synagogue that provided the bases for Christian worship.*

In synagogue worship, the *emphasis was not on sacrifice but on prayers, the reading of the Psalms and the Prophets, and an exposition of the set Scriptures.* In other words, Word and Prayer. (These scriptural lessons were read according to a seasonal pattern and written down in a lectionary.) The use of a seasonal lectionary is still standard in type-two services. What we see is that worship of the first century incorporated the elements of Word plus sacrifice.

William Maxwell incorporates the meaning of synagogue and temple as being the eschatological celebration of Christ's sacrifice during a meal in the upper room. So many speak of the roots of Christian worship as being the *worship of the synagogue coupled with the (now-completed) sacrificial emphasis of worship of the temple.*[35]

Is Our Worship Biblical?

It may surprise many of my type-one friends to hear that nowhere in the Bible, or anywhere in the entire history of the church, do we find reference to any other form of worship service other than that of Holy Communion (or whatever other name is applied. e.g., the breaking of bread, Acts 2:42). In other words, every first day of the week, Christians did not meet for a service with a lot of singing, followed by a lot of preaching! There was only one celebration. It was the worship Jesus commanded. Sunday morning was a celebration of a banquet. It was an anticipation of the eternal banquet to which we are all invited. (Later, for reasons such as we see in 1 Cor. 11:17–22, the meal was dropped.) By His sacrifice, it was an amazing celebration of Christ's victory in *redemption* and of His victory in our eternal *restoration.*

William Francis, in his book, *Celebrate the Feasts of the Lord,* draws our attention to the connection of the major Jewish feasts with their fulfillment in Christ. The Feast of First Fruits (16th of Nisan) is a celebration of Christ's restoration in all who are connected to His resurrection. Our connection to Jesus, the first fruits from the dead (1 Cor. 15:23), is also our first day of the week of new creation.[36] What else

---

35   William D. Maxwell, *An Outline of Christian Worship.* (London: Oxford University Press, 1960), 5.

36   William W. Francis, *Celebrate the Feasts of the Lord.* (Alexandria, VA: Crest Books, Salvation Army Pub., 1993), 47.

should we celebrate when we come together on that day? The resurrection of Jesus calls us to look to the first day of new creation.

Not surprisingly, liturgies have been handed down throughout the history of the church, or at least we may see them from the period of Justin Martyr's rite (approximately AD 140). We don't have a record of any other prior to this rite. One reason may be because there was a great diversity of practices throughout the whole church. Also, the services were never rigid. There was form, but it was loose and depended on a lot of improvisation on commonly understood forms.

In the second century, we are rapidly approaching a time when flexibility in worship disappeared. Ralph Martin, a scholar and a leading figure in the Roman Catholic Charismatic Movement, adds this: "The day of the spontaneously offered worship in which all the members of the congregation share at will (as in 1Corinthians 14) is over; and we are approaching the era of service-books and liturgies."[37]

The late Evelyn Underhill, the great historian and liturgist, refers to the church's earlier period in this way:

> And it is here, perhaps, that we find our best clue to the character of Christian Eucharistic worship at the close of the first century, when the primitive and un-stylized experience of the Apostolic Church was losing its apocalyptic character and beginning to assume a ritual form … but there was little desire to enclose this sacred experience within the bounds of a rigid formula, or define the precise means by which it was assured.[38]

What a smart first-century church! They believed in the Trinity but refused to articulate it. They believed in the real presence in Communion but didn't define it. But they did understand *spiritual realities*. In the beginning, the Word said, "Let there be," and there was. At the last

---

37   Ralph P. Martin, *Worship in the Early Church*. (Grand Rapids, MI: Eerdman's Pub., 1974), 139.

38   Evelyn Underhill, *Worship*. (New York: Crossroad Pub. Co., 1982), 239.

supper, they believed, "It is," because Jesus, the Word, said so. "This is my body ... this is my blood." The apostle Paul put it like this:

> Is not the cup of thanksgiving for which we give thanks a participation in the blood of Christ? And is not the bread that we break a participation in the body of Christ? Because there is one loaf, we, who are many, are one body, for we all partake of the one loaf. (1Cor.10:16)

Likewise, the Apostle John, who does not record the Last Supper, quotes Jesus in relation to His teaching on the Bread of Life:

> Very truly, I tell you, unless you eat the flesh of the Son of Man and drink his blood, you have no life in you. Those who eat my flesh and drink my blood have eternal life, and I will raise them up on the last day; for my flesh is true food and my blood is true drink. (John 6:53-55)

Ralph Martin notes, "The real presence tends, from this point of the development onwards, to be located not in a spiritual reception of Christ by faith, but in the elements themselves."[39] From Thomas Aquinas to Martin Luther to John Calvin to Thomas Cranmer to John Knox, we see a variety of opinions ranging from the real presence to the real absence of Christ. No words can explain mystery. They may explain magic! But when the Word says something, then it is what He says *because He said so!* It is something more than a subjective spiritual experience. The entire action of receiving bread and wine is sometimes spoken of as something of a sacramental nature, because Jesus is involved in it. *He spoke; we received!* Of course, the word *sacrament* is more usually associated with the second type. In one denomination, sacrament is described as, "An outward and visible sign of an inward and spiritual grace ... a means whereby we receive this grace, and a pledge to assure us thereof."[40] (For a little fuller treatment on this topic of Holy Communion, you may want to refer to my book *Time and the Biblical Bang*.)

---

39 Martin, *Worship in the Early Church*, 139.

40 *Book of Common Prayer*, The Anglican Church of Canada, 1962, 550.

Certainly, improvisation was a key element in the worship of the apostolic period. Nevertheless, it is easy to observe that its liturgy provided a sense of *movement* between essential elements of the celebration. At one church I mentioned my little hypothesis, "If the twelve apostles were to drop in here right now, they wouldn't recognize this service as Christian worship." The type-one congregation was totally shocked. "How dare Charles suggest that what we are doing isn't biblical." After a careful explanation, people lined up to thank me for my *very biblical* sermon.

Does Our Worship Move in a Direction?

Evelyn Underhill seems to be thankful when acknowledging that the church gradually moved beyond the "spontaneous elements in common worship." However, by the middle of the second century, it had *not* moved very far. Thankfully! (That's my sentiment. However, the inclusion of informality didn't stay that way for long!) Underhill notes the following principle of formality interspersed with informality:

> Early in the second century, Justin Martyr describes an ordered service of prayer, psalms, Scripture reading, a sermon, directly derived from synagogue sources and practically identical in character with the later Liturgy of the Catechumens.[41]

Incidentally, the catechumens were those who were being prepared for baptism into the faith. (Today we might call them seekers). At one stage, they left the service as it moved into *the mysteries* of the bread and wine. In *The Didache* (an ancient book of teachings, and possibly written around AD 100), this admonition is noted: "During or at the end of the meal, the unbaptized are warned not to participate 'of your Eucharist.'"[42] Once they arrived at this point, these people left the group of worshipers. They had not yet received enough preparation to meet with the Lord in the awesome mystery of Communion. To this point,

---

41   Underhill, *Worship*, 240.

42   Kleist, *The Didache*, 7.

they had participated in the synagogue forms of prayer, the Psalms, the Law and Prophets, and the sermon. Underhill goes on:

> Nevertheless extempore and 'prophetic' prayer, as the voice of the Spirit, was still preferred to any liturgical formula, especially in the Eucharist. The celebrant who was unable to present the 'collected prayer' of the faithful in his own words was held in some contempt, and at least until the end of the second century even the great Eucharistic Prayer appears to have had no fixed or obligatory form ... for Eucharistic worship is above all an action, partly human and partly divine.[43]

Some may feel somewhat disappointed that most *post-first-century* people seemed to feel more comfortable trusting primarily in their own efforts and theological language. Underhill also seems to share a certain discomfort in trusting the spontaneity of the Spirit's leading. All the Spirit wants to do is, in an orderly way, to take us corporately beyond ourselves and into the mystery of transcendence. But that attitude of wariness appears to have become the norm in both types of *contemporary* church life: structure and worship. Should we not expect to meet with the awesome God who longs to reveal His presence? I'm for form *and* spontaneity in the Spirit! With a discerning president of worship, we really can trust where the Holy Spirit wants to take us (1 Cor. 14:39–40).

Of course, what is happening, beyond the ministry of the Word, are elements of movement designed to celebrate the mysteries as the apostle Paul says, "in a worthy manner."

> Therefore, whoever eats the bread or drinks the cup of the Lord in an unworthy manner will be guilty of sinning against the body and blood of the Lord. A man ought to examine himself before he eats of the bread and drinks of the cup. For anyone who eats and drinks without recognizing the body eats and drinks judgment on himself. (1 Cor. 11:27–29)

---

43   Underhill, *Worship*, 240.

I must confess that sometimes, in our wanderings, I was uncomfortable with the casual way an elder sometimes offered these elements of bread and wine to the congregation. Anyone who wants to receive them is not prevented. Mostly, there was no call to repentance before we received God's gifts to us. We need to be called to a manner in which we may accept the gifts *worthily*, and that is particularly important when a person enters a Christian service for the first time. How can that person, appearing with a well-meaning friend, have been prepared for this awesome mystery? The first-century church knew what it was doing!

Receiving the bread and wine (that is set apart for this purpose) is a lot more than a method to remember the meaning of the cross. I don't need to go to church to remember Calvary. My own sin reminds me of that every day! Passing the bread and wine along the row to those who have come to God on their own terms, or those ignorant of the need to get right with God, is just not good enough, *and it's not biblical or historical!* That goes for all types of churches. Please read the amazing parable Jesus told of the man who came to the wedding feast on his own terms (Matt. 22:1–14). Surely none of us can feast at God's banquet on our own terms. Here is one of the wonderful elements (individual and corporate confession) of a form that helps us prepare to meet the gracious awesomeness of God. Speaking of the mysticism of the apostle Paul, Evelyn Underhill might agree.

> He is the unique link between the primitive apostolic experiences of communion with the Risen Jesus and the still-continued Christo-centric mysticism of the Church; and might with some justice be called both the first of Evangelicals and first of Catholics.[44]

Repeating Familiar Words

There are some of the type-one persuasion who tell us that *repeating words* strip them of all meaning. Let me offer a couple of reasons why I heartily

---

44 Evelyn Underhill, *Mystics of the Church*. (Cambridge: James Clarke & Co, 1975), 39.

disagree. If you were to ask me, "What is twelve multiplied by six?" I wouldn't rush for my calculator. Immediately, I would answer, "Seventy-two." Why is that? It's because at school, I was taught to memorize the twelve times table. It comes naturally to me now. (Maybe I'll get the other tables one day!)

My mother died at ninety-six. Two years prior to this, we could hold a truncated conversation about the past or the present. She had a great sense of humor, but it all went by somewhere. Because of accelerating dementia, she never remembered our common past. All we had was the present moment. Once I saw her just five minutes after my brother, Allan, had visited her. Having talked with Allan as he departed, my first question to Mum was, "Have you seen Allan lately?" Mum replied, "No, I haven't seen him for a long time." However, when I prayed with my mother, I always included the Lord's Prayer. That day, as she did every day, she vocalized every single word of it.

We can put down both instances to subliminal learning. The Jews were subliminal learners. Ask a male Jewish believer the meaning of his Bar Mitzvah. He will easily tell you of his identity in the faith of his fathers. How did the psalmist put it?

> I have hidden your word in my heart that I might not sin against you. (Ps. 119:11)

We are called to live naturally the meaning of our faith that lies subliminally within us. Clearly, the psalmist is here acknowledging that his thinking and actions are very much shaped by the word of the Lord. It is *subliminally guiding the decisions* he faces in his daily life. The Jews were a subliminal people! At my age, I am very grateful that I made a concerted effort to memorize Scripture.

To say that the repetition of words robs them of their meaning is a denial of the normal ways in which we conduct our life. Every time I get into the driver's seat of my car, I don't make the effort to recall all my driving lessons. For Verna, that's obvious! It's not all based on feelings! Ask the makers of television commercials! The fact that you may be saying liturgical words without any feeling or emotion on a particular day is really quite unimportant. (It's a bit like speaking in tongues. You don't wait for a feeling; you speak in tongues as a matter of the will.)

The fact is, for the vast majority of my type-two churches, their liturgy literally drips with biblical phrases. Words that you said last Sunday (whether you thought of them or not) have now impregnated your life. They are there right now, guiding and shaping your decisions. *Good liturgy helps us to think biblically.* Nevertheless, it's great to feel those words next Sunday! I know the Lord's Prayer shapes my thoughts day after day. However, I don't remember getting excited about saying it with Verna this morning. Joining with others in repeating liturgical phrases declares you to be part of not only a worshipping community but also a historical people of a common memory.

Creeds, such as the Apostles' Creed or the Nicene Creed, had not yet been formulated in the first century. Indeed, they were not generally in use for several hundred years. However, most scholars agree that the biblical basis for them had already been written down in a variety of baptismal formulae.[45] Ralph Martin notes that we can see some of these statements in biblical passages such as Acts 16:31–33, Ephesians 5:25–26, and Philippians 2:6–11.[46] The result of such baptismal confessions has been that, in their worship services, congregations have joined together to confess *one universal faith.* In other words, when a Baptist congregation repeats the Apostles' Creed somewhere in Texas, they are declaring the one faith with a CSI congregation in South India. Indeed, the apostle Paul may have further contributed to this universal confession in the words, "One Lord, one faith, one baptism, one God and Father of all" (Eph. 4:5).

Of course, there is another form of confession: *confession of sin* before the people approach the banqueting table. In some traditions, the people are invited to leave their places for a very good reason. It signifies that a person has left behind his or her past sin and failure. Then he or she may come forward in freedom and deliverance. As Paul says, come "worthily" to the table of the Lord (1 Cor. 11:27).

---

45   Maxwell, *An Outline of Christian Worship*, 38.

46   Martin, *Worship in the Early Church*, 61.

Usually when people make a confession of their sin (either in personal silence and privacy or in corporate words of confession), they are thinking in personal and individual terms. However, confession is intended to be more than that. What about the things to which God has called the congregation but that have never been done? So confession is both individual and corporate in nature.

Music in Worship

Music is a powerful element in expressing praise and adoration to God. On our *pilgrimage*, the number of churches that currently use music groups to lead worship surprised us. In our type-two churches, that little job had traditionally been reserved for an organist and a choir. It's an age of diversity, so we must allow for the fact that the aesthetic value of music is also diverse. As a lover of classical and jazz music, I can appreciate such variety. (I try to play jazz piano because I improvise and no knows I am playing it wrongly. Classical music also lends itself to improvisation, but I can't play it!) Maybe that's why I like worship to have diversity of form, of improvisation, of spiritual revelation, of silence, and of familiar words that take me beyond myself. *Liturgy, crowded with words, may easily bore me. Lesser liturgy, comprising of a lot of singing, followed by a lot of preaching, may be equally boring!*

The fact is the church has always written music that is understood in the popular milieu. King David composed simple modal music that was designed for folk worship. In medieval times, Renaissance music offered the modal forms sung by the ordinary person. John Merbeck's sixteenth-century plain song music was intended for the common person. In many churches, his chants are still used. However, I want to pass on some observations concerning how music is led in churches that observe significant time for intentional worship.

Worship Leader and/or Song Leader?

In almost every situation I have encountered in the last few years, it has been very rare to witness worship led by what I would call a worship leader. More likely, in my opinion, the leader may best be described as a song leader. There is nothing wrong with that, but a song leader plays a different role than one who is leading the worship time.

Usually in a block of time devoted to worship, the song leader takes control of about six to eight songs (sometimes it goes on longer). These songs have been previously chosen and rehearsed. A good song leader will be very careful in presenting these songs in an order that moves. For example, personally, I always differentiate between praise songs and worship songs. In between are one or two bridge songs.

Praise songs are those that speak *about* God while worship songs are those that speak *to* God; they are usually songs of adoration. In the praise songs (especially these days), the words are often loaded with personal pronouns: "I, I, I," or "we, we, we." They can be forgiven in the praise songs. And that's because a lot of these songs not only thank God for what He has done for us but declare what He means to us. These are songs that lend themselves to shouts, bodily movement, and lots of clapping. They are songs like "Shout to the Lord" or "Ah, Lord God."

Participation through Praise Songs

Praise songs prove to be wonderful opportunities to allow for short, personal testimonies of thanksgiving. Here, between songs, the leader may make a short comment on the song and then ask if anyone wants to thank God for something of recent importance. In my own experience, this sharing has been a wonderful time of informality and joy. Of course, someone should be there to ensure the speaker has a microphone. But the speaker doesn't hold the microphone. The leader, who holds the microphone, also discretely withdraws it. At the discernment of the leader, two to three minutes of short thanksgiving is usually enough! Sometimes informal prayer breaks out for one or two of the persons who have spoken.

Bridge songs (one or two) may do the same (i.e., "Change My Heart, Oh God," or Selah's "We Press On"), but they definitely begin to change the tone and the focus. They are leading to what Matt Redmond entitled one song as, "The Heart of Worship." (Incidentally, the theme phrase, "It's all about You," was the first song written by Redmond after he stopped writing them. He was fed up with supposed worship music that spoke more of us than they did about God. About five years later, he was determined to write worship songs that spoke of Him, alone).

Worship songs are all *about and to Him*. They are sung to think of nothing but being in His presence. I think of songs like "Majesty" or "Glorify Thy Name." This is definitely not music that consists of four or five verses. We are not here engaged in a cerebral exercise of theological thought but a Spirit-to-spirit engagement of awe in God. It becomes very natural to move into corporate singing in tongues or singing spontaneously around a chord in the native tongue. Actually, there may also be times when, even in the praise section, it seems natural, as Paul says, to "sing with the spirit" (1 Cor. 14:15).

A Common Problem

There were times when Verna and I (when visiting churches) thought we were in worship and moving quite naturally into spiritual manifestations. But they very rarely ever happened. Indeed, we were surprised in many Pentecostal churches to note that there was little or nothing that happened of a charismatic nature. There was a lot of singing with a lot of preaching! *We have become a passive culture that's petrified by silence.*

> But the Lord is in his holy temple. Let all the earth be silent before him. (Hab. 2:20)

In many churches, the congregation expects to be passively moved by someone or something else. But I would say that, sometimes, the most significant problem preventing the Holy Spirit from manifesting His gifts are musicians. They don't know when to *shut up*! Being something of an amateur musician, and having had a lot of experience in leading worship, I understand how hard it is for a musician to lay down his instrument. But why are we afraid of silence?

When we have been singing in the Spirit or singing our love to God in the vernacular, it is so natural to wait upon His presence to move us. On a vast number of occasions, a guitarist or pianist constantly playing a major chord and its relative minor absolutely ruined the silence. Predictably, even a very short silence was broken by a musician. An instrument had to break the silence. The worship leader (who may not be one of the musicians) will not allow this, but a song leader probably will. Please, please, allow the Spirit to manifest words of knowledge or prophecy, or whatever He wills, *in the silence, which is a coveted part of worship.*

Personally, I have great difficulty with those who condescendingly look down their noses at churches where emotion is allowed. Often such people will speak of the music as "ditties." Or they might say, "Where decent music is used, that sort of thing will never happen." While I was at St. James' Church, Calgary, we employed a first-class organist and choir master. He did a wonderful job. Not long after hearing a beautiful anthem, often we would break into singing in tongues. Most people came to appreciate a variety of worship music. Personally, I was equally ecstatic with a diversity of musical forms. Wouldn't the person speaking only of classical forms also have some sense of emotion in church while listening to Stainer's "Crucifixion" or Handel's "Hallelujah Chorus"? Surely the entire focus is to be in the presence of God. I think that's often emotional too! But that leads us to the worship leader. I must confess that sometimes when I tell Verna how much I love her, I actually feel it!

Worship Leader

This leader may not always be a gifted musician who plays an instrument. However, the worship leader is up front with the musicians and with a microphone. This person, if not one of the musicians, should definitely have some knowledge of music; will lead singing in the Spirit; should have the gift of discernment of the Spirit; discernment of what is not of the Spirit; sensitivity of where the Spirit is leading; possess the courage to move with the Spirit; may or may not be an experienced clergyperson; and will exercise boldness in applying Scriptural admonitions:

1. Two or three should speak at the most, and ensure that there is an interpretation (1 Cor. 14:27).

2. Ensure that there is no confusion while people are giving a revelation. For example, when two or more want to speak at the same time, or when a person wants to speak at an inappropriate point in the service (such as when someone is reading a Scripture

lesson). "The spirits of prophets are subject to the control of prophets" (1 Cor. 14:32). In other words, someone has to shut up!

3. "God is a God not of disorder but peace" (v. 33). "But everything should be done in a fitting and orderly way" (v. 40).

I recall one time when our Anglican Renewal Movement was holding a large conference at Carlton University, Ottawa. At the previous national board meeting, we agreed upon a very fine group of musicians to lead the singing. However, I asked if the leader was gifted in moving with the Spirit. Few seemed to know. One or two thought it would be fine. At our opening service in the Anglican cathedral, the leader asked if anyone wanted to speak. As a result, about fourteen people lined up behind the microphone. Every person was allowed to speak. Much of it was repetitious, and a lot of it was not at all edifying (1 Cor. 14:26). Fortunately, there were a few powerful messages from God. However, the service went on so long that many had trouble getting back to hotels that night!

Sometimes when I led the worship at St. James', I noticed why spiritual gifts and other revelations seemed to come more naturally after we had sung in tongues. It seemed to unlock the things God wanted to do and show us. At such times, God led us to minister to situations He revealed. However, in general, most people understood their message could be delivered in two or three minutes. Someone would take the mike to a person standing at the end of a row. Then he would hold on to it and politely take it from a person's mouth as he or she quickly signed off. There were times when a person was clearly speaking from a personal agenda or saying something that seemed to be unbiblical. Of course, the person was never told that his revelation was wrong. A worship leader, sensitive to the feelings of that person, would simply say to the congregation, "Please pray to God for what He wants you to know right now." Most people realized the message may be questionable.

Having mentioned that there may be problems, I suspect that some church leaders will be tempted to close down any of those possibilities. Once people have received the laying on of hands, after teaching on the work of the Spirit, there must be opportunity to exercise spiritual gifts in normal situations. It's very simple, really. *If we don't risk questionable situations from people, we will never enjoy great revelations from the Spirit.*

> Therefore, my brothers, be eager to prophesy, and do not forbid speaking in tongues. But everything should be done in a fitting and orderly way. (1 Cor. 14:39–40)

I would love to show you a form of worship I have put together. For reasons stated above, it will not be exactly what would have been used in first-century worship. Nevertheless, the major principles and movement are there. *Form plus informal movement of the Spirit is strongly encouraged.* Bold statements of a universal faith had not yet been formed, but a Creed is included here. First-century folk singing is not included, but the service definitely encourages contemporary music. It's my personal preference that we don't lose the great hymns of the church. Some songs should never be sung twice, while music that has proven its worth in bringing people into the heart of God is worthy, whether it is two weeks old or two hundred years. That's the criteria: Does it bring people into the presence of God?

Principles of Early Christian Worship

An Opening Hymn or Song
In some churches, children and youth proceed to their classes.

The Gathering
The presiding elder opens the gathering with a welcome to the congregation, and to the visitors. There is a verbal invitation to worship (may include Ps. 100:4, John 4:24, or other Scriptures).

The Ministry of the Word
A reader prays a short prayer of thanks for the theme of today's Scripture readings.

Reader (after an Old Testament reading or a New Testament Letter):
This is the Word of the Lord.

People: Thanks be to God.

Reader: Leads the reading of a Psalm (sometimes a Passover psalm of deliverance, e.g., Psalms 113–118).

The Gospel Reading (*from one of the four gospels*)
Reader (after the gospel reading): This is the gospel of Christ.

People: Thanks be to God.

The Creed
Standing, all say the Apostles' Creed or the Nicene Creed.

The Sermon may be delivered here or after
songs of praise and worship.

Songs of Praise and Worship
In some churches, children and youth join the rest of the congregation for singing and participating in spiritual gifts ministries. After or during,

the praise songs (songs about God), about *three people* may share current testimonies of thanksgivings (for no more than two to three minutes per person).

Worship songs (songs to God) may lead to "singing with the spirit" (1 Cor. 14:15). There should be *total silence after worship singing*. Words of revelation may follow, which may also lead to immediate ministry. Otherwise ministry may be given through anointed ministry teams, now or at the end of the service.

Offerings

Hymn or Song of Offering. The offerings and thanksgivings are then brought to the elder or deacon, who offers an informal prayer of thanksgiving.

Offerings of Intercession. The congregation is led by an elder or another person who invites the people to offer *one-sentence prayers* for the following, or other concerns:

+ The wider church of God

+ Those in leadership in our country and the world

+ Peace in war and for those in distress

+ The poor and all those who are broken

+ Those who are lost without Christ

+ Those who are sick or in any kind of need

+ For God's help in our church ministries

Entering the Mystery of Presence in Repentance

Presiding Elder: The Lord Jesus invites us to feast at the eternal banquet He has prepared for us. In repentance and faith, we come to You, oh God. We invite You to search our hearts to reveal those things preventing us from entering the mystery of Your holiness and grace.

As individuals, we confess to God: (*A short time of silence*).

As a congregation, we confess to God: (*A short time of silence*)

Presiding Elder: "If we say that we have no sin, we deceive ourselves, and the truth is not in us. If we confess our sins, he who is faithful and just will forgive us our sins and cleanse us from all unrighteousness" (1 John 1:8–9).

We receive our forgiveness in the name of Jesus Christ. By His grace, we are free! Amen!

People: *Hallelujah!*

Presiding Elder: Brothers and sisters, let us share the peace of Christ with those around us.

The people greet each other: Words may be used, such as, "The peace of Christ be with you." A hymn or song of worship may be sung.

The Great Thanksgiving

In an informal or formal prayer, the presiding elder gives thanks for this eternal banquet and for:

1. The gift of salvation in Jesus,

2. The resurrection of Jesus and His coming again in glory.

3. The gift of redemption and restoration through Christ's offering of new creation's fruit of innocence.

People: (Said or sung) Holy, holy, holy Lord God of power and might. Heaven and earth are full of Your glory. Hosanna in the highest.

A hymn or song of worship may be sung.

Consecration: In the Words of the Word

Presiding Elder: Lord Jesus, we recall that, on the night You were handed over to death, You took bread, and when You had given thanks, You broke it and said, "This is my body, which is given for you; do this in remembrance of me" (Luke 22:19).

When the supper was over, You took the cup of blessing, and after giving thanks, You said, "This cup that is poured out is the new covenant in my blood" (Luke 22:20). Thank you that this fruit of creation is the remembrance of our redemption from the state of the fall and of our restoration in this feast of holy innocence. We pray that by the power of the Holy Spirit, we may be filled with Your grace and heavenly blessings. Amen.

People: God—Father, Son, and Holy Spirit—through these gifts of bread and wine, bless us in the promise of Your presence. Enable us to share with others the risen life of Jesus Christ, who is Lord of all.

Presiding Elder: Together, we share this mystery of faith:

People: Christ has died. Christ is risen. Christ will come again. Hallelujah!

Elder: As Jesus taught us, so we say together:

> Our Father in heaven, hallowed be Your name. Your kingdom come, Your will be done, on earth as in heaven. Give us today our daily bread. Forgive us our sin as we forgive those who sin against us. Save us in times of temptation, and deliver us from evil. For the kingdom, the

power, and the glory are Yours, now and forever. Amen.

Presiding Elder: Come to the Lord's table and in thankfulness, receive these gifts of Christ's innocent fruits of redemption and restoration.

Individually, the person administering the bread may say: Take and eat this in remembrance that Christ died for you.

Individually, the person administering the cup may say: Drink this in remembrance that Christ's blood was shed for you.

In some churches, the words are: The body of Christ given for you. The blood of Christ shed for you.

After the bread and wine have been distributed, the remains are discretely consumed. An elder or deacon may receive some of the elements that are to be taken to the sick or the elderly. During this time, musicians may lead with songs of thanksgiving.

Elder: Let us bless the Lord for all His goodness to us. In the power of the Spirit, be a sign of new creation, in the love of God the Father, God the Son, and God the Holy Spirit.
People: Glory to God forever and ever. Amen.

A Closing Song or Hymn
At the end of the service, an elder or deacon says:
Go in peace to love and serve the Lord.
People: Thanks be to God. Hallelujah!

CHAPTER 9

The Big Picture

There is no doubt that the first-century church consisted of group-based, house communities. By now, of course, you may realize I am not speaking of a program-based church with home groups. I refer exclusively to a church that has as its very base and foundation a number of groups. The usual place for these biweekly meetings is in houses. *It was the groups that formed the basis for entrance into the church community, and it was the groups that produced a structure of encouragement of leadership and of a governing council.*

When I was ministering in Calgary and Victoria, and while I was encouraging the use of home groups, I had not encountered anything else but a program church with home groups included. I think Ralph Neighbour's Touch Ministry's resources spurred me to look even further. However, I often wondered why the church with groups had not set the Western world afire. In the Western world, I never really thought of churches operating without church buildings. Buildings are and can be an enormous benefit to church life, when used wisely. However, the absence of a church building need not hinder the growth and nurture of the church. We are not yet in a position where we have to operate in the way Chinese Christians are forced to minister. Yet the growth in that country must be as exciting as it was in the first-century church.

In the second century, there may have been a number of buildings that were used for church gatherings, but I believe the first church building to operate solely as a church facility did not appear until about the year AD 250 in Syria. Therefore, the most basic form of the church, as it developed through the apostles and evangelists, would have looked something like this:

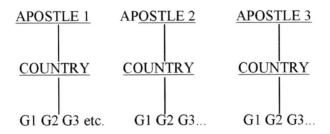

G1, G2, G3, etc., represent a number of *house groups* established in each country. Not surprisingly, the New Testament often alludes to these house-type churches. Luke makes it very clear that the places where they worshipped (and developed growth in discipleship) took place in the houses of ordinary people (Acts 2:41–46; 5:42). Whether we speak of Jerusalem, Antioch, Ephesus, Rome, or wherever, it's very clear that *the small group was the most practical way in which to engage in making disciples and to grow in numbers.*

Indeed, the home group was the primary entrance point to the life of the church community. Bringing people to a church service, as the first point of contact, most likely would not have been the first point of contact with the community. In fact, I would venture a typical scenario. Your Bible version may be different than mine, but I think this is the real story. In Acts 2, after his anointing with the Spirit, we see that Peter preached his first post-Pentecost sermon.

He stood at the edge of a river or a pool with his laptop in his hand. As people emerged from the waters of baptism, he would say, "Philip and Naomi, you go to Joe and Lydia's house next Tuesday at 7:00 p.m." Then he would enter it into his database, and Philip and Naomi showed up at Joe and Lydia's house on Tuesday. How else were those apostles going to deal with the newly-baptized who lived nearby?

Paul refers to the church in the house of Nympha (Col. 4:15), of Archippus (Phil. 2), of Chloe (1 Cor. 1:11), and of Prisca and Aquilla (Rom.16:5). Who knows where they met for worship on Sundays! (That's if, at the beginning, all gatherings actually did meet on Sundays.) They met together in caves, on beaches, in forests, or anywhere they could get peace and quiet. For some it would have been on their way to work! As we see, the *direction of ministry*, proceeding from the life and nature of the Trinity, is anything but hierarchical or centralized. We shall see later how the foundations of apostolic ministry are built upon Jesus Christ in *relational ways*.

> I left you behind in Crete for this reason, so that you should put in order what remained to be done, and should appoint elders in every town, as I directed you. (Titus 1:5)

From our observation of Paul's commission to Titus, we note a number of things. They remind us of what may well be the structure and priorities in the Pauline churches. Indeed, *nearly all the churches* mentioned in the New Testament appeared to emulate the structure of a synagogue, with elders as the governing order.

In chapter 1, we note that Paul refers to those who will be the leaders of churches as elders (Titus 1:5). For him, the same people are also bishops or overseers (v. 7 and Acts 20:17, 28). Clearly the leadership of each church lay in the ministry of the elders. Some leaders were to be *appointed* as elders by Titus.

I have a broad idea of what Paul wanted, having travelled across the length of Crete, which is about 150 miles. The height, from top to bottom, would average between twenty to twenty-five miles. I realize it would be difficult for Titus to know who those elders should be. I imagine, shortly after the beginning, there could easily have been about fifteen to twenty churches on the island. Of course, Titus was with Paul as churches were being founded, but it would still be difficult to choose the right leaders for every place. He must have been a powerful praying man!

Paul and Titus may have had some idea who the leaders should be. However, the aid of local *affirmation* would also be very useful. *In the groups, spiritual and natural gifts would become apparent.* Others would be recognized in groups that aligned themselves as one local church in one location. Local, prayerful people, with the knowledge of their groups, would be able to affirm who the elders (with their different gifts) may be. One might be gifted in administration, one in teaching, one in apostolic church planting, one in pastoral ministry, etc. *Through prayer, consultation, and affirmation,* Titus, like James in Jerusalem, would then be better equipped to choose the elders for each place. In local charismatic churches of today, clergy and other people lay hands on affirmed people and release them into local areas of ministry.

Paul had also given guidelines concerning the character and abilities of these leaders. Titus 1:5–8 speaks of their character and life style. Verse 9 speaks of their ability to understand the faith "in accordance with the teaching … so that he may be able both to preach with sound doctrine and to refute those who contradict it." In other words, the *elders* would be capable guardians of the apostolic faith.

The case for an unbroken apostolic chain of succession through the laying on of hands appears to be more obscure or sporadic here than in later times. Paul was not one of the twelve (although he believed that he had demonstrated apostolic credentials [2 Cor. 12:12] and was not inferior to the "superlative apostles" He may have had in mind Peter, James and John. Mark 9:2) Titus, in his oversight, was most certainly not a monarchical bishop in a later Ignatian sense. He may have been recognized as an evangelist or one involved in apostolic ministry (i.e., in church-planting and building the embryonic church community). It seems that, to Paul, the criterion for apostolic credibility did not lie strictly in a much-later recognition of succession, but it certainly did include signs and wonders, plus the ability to guard the apostolic faith. *In the New Testament, titles are not about institutional status but are related to spiritual gifting, so bishop as an order of ministry did not appear in the first century at all!* No wonder the succeeding church, with institutional condescension, refers to it as the primitive church.

Although we see some similarities, we cannot say the Pauline structure of ministry was exactly the same as that in Jerusalem. *And that's precisely the point. There was a diversity of form.* Clearly, James is recognized as the leader in the Jerusalem community. That's the way Eusebius, the fourth-century historian, saw James. He referred to him as the "archon" or leader of the church in Jerusalem. (After this pattern, I refer to a primary elder of a church community as being the *leading elder*.) Despite some Orthodox and Roman claims, none of the twelve apostles ever held that place. Apostles were called to establish churches, not to be resident managers of them. We see that the Titus example bears out the point. The overseers (who were elders) held oversight of a church or territory.

Ignatius seems to be the first person to claim the exclusive and monarchical role of oversight in a community (about AD 107). For a while, some of the twelve used Jerusalem as their base of outreach. Others, like John or Andrew, quite quickly established their apostolic roles in distant places. In Jerusalem, it was the elders who were the governors. Here, as in a few places, like Philippi, deacons had been appointed for a ministry of service in feeding the poor. (The Greek word *diakonos* means "to serve." Later deacons also took on a serving role at the celebration of Holy Communion.)

What about Today?

I mention this fuller introduction because there is a resurgence of group-based and house churches today. For some, the authority to pioneer and structure their lives in this way was not sought in particular denominations. These group churches are growing and often demonstrate powerful evidence of the apostolic signs, as outlined above. Quite probably all the churches on the island of Crete maintained their independence while uniting in a fellowship of churches upholding the apostolic faith. Crete may well provide a very good model toward which many churches of the future are headed. (Indeed, it would be my dream to see a Fellowship of First-Century Christian Churches. Imagine, once entrance requirements had been set, how it may be to see local groups of independent and denominational churches in a given area or wider who are accountable to each other and supportive of one another.)

Maybe we can learn something that is pertinent to our quest from a variety of New Testament forms! In a somewhat paradoxical way, we also see the influence of forms such as those begun in Jerusalem. Clearly, in the first century, a time came when the apostles had either died or had ventured far beyond Jerusalem, their starting point. However, the focus of churches, far and wide, was not on an individual person but on the apostolic faith understood and defended in the whole apostolic community. Apostolic life and character were obviously exercised and expected in the five points that were earlier outlined.

The fact is, while many mainline churches of the West are watering down the gospel in their haste to act as chaplains to the culture, Christians of the global south speak and live prophetically to their cultures. Various cultures really do need a bigger worldview that looks to transcendence, hope, and meaning. Having encountered the prophetic voice, consequently, thousands upon thousands now speak of values in a person. They know Jesus in living and intimate terms.

They speak of lives that have been transformed not only through a tradition of right teaching but by their introduction to a life of right relationships! They know life through Jesus!

Entry Level: The Home Group

As we have seen previously, throughout the world, the most significant growth of the church is being experienced in group or house-based communities. I believe the dying church of the West shows the most need of following after this direction. We can't die while comforting ourselves that we did so by maintaining our individual traditions. And most, if not all, of the traditions have well fallen short of a loyalty to first-century principles. The label "primitive church" did nothing to help!

In this present generation, I have realized a simple principle. Generally, people pursue relationships without being captivated by institutions. However, I really don't think we can be naïve concerning institutions. Didn't Jesus once say, "Wherever two or three are gathered together in My name, there is an institution"? I agree; He didn't say that. But the fact is we are naturally institutional. It's not a case of ideology without institution but what kind of institution? Surely, it is one that best models the character and purpose of the kingdom of God. I am inviting the church to reconsider the elephantine institutions that consume all too much of our time and resources. All too often, in those situations, national councils set the agenda for the way local churches spend their mission offerings. The result often means resources for ministry at the local level are considerably exploited. Becoming a gifted and relational people who sign the life of Eden cannot be compromised. *First-century principles are excellent criteria for signing the meaning of Eden in a twenty-first-century world.*

For these and other reasons, most un-churched people would be far more open to an invitation to a home than to a church. Often people say that in a church service, there are many traditions and styles to be overcome when they are introduced to a community through a worship service first. (And that includes the mention of a chasm that exists between the culture of the world and that of Christian worship). We may have to accept that some people may never be comfortable in a formal Sunday-morning church service. Some churches juggle around with what days may be best to invite people to church. However, I firmly believe it would be easier to introduce people to community by inviting them first to a home group and then to the larger church.

I made a mistake once, I think! After I shared my faith in Jesus with a used car salesman, he agreed to come to church the following Sunday. It was one of those Sundays when an issue of church life just had to be addressed. It did nothing for him! Guess where he wasn't the next week? He told me that the particular sermon—an essential part of that worshipping congregation for that time—was not important enough to draw him back! It would have been better had I taken a different approach with him. *I should have invited him to a home group first! Although our friends may not come with us to church, there's a very good possibility they will meet with a group of people in our home.*

Many people are accustomed to groups today! Lots of them have been in AA, Single Mothers, or some kind of self-help group. (That used car salesman was already used to groups; he was a member of AA.)

Following is an interesting set of statistics.[47] These stats are all about the old-fashioned way of first trying to get people to come to church. When we compare the approaches, we learn one thing: the most effective evangelism is good, old-fashioned friendship!

HOW PEOPLE ARE BROUGHT INTO THE CHURCH	
By Advertisement	2%
By the Pastor	6%
By Organized Evangelistic Outreach	6%
By Friends and Relatives	86%

Wow—86 percent of people are brought in by friends and relatives! Today can you imagine what would happen if that 86 percent turned their invitations to bringing people to a house where about six plus people offer a warm welcome? There is no need to start learning a ritual in that house! The Greek New Testament uses the word *oikos* quite a lot. An oikos is a house, but the word can also be used to mean household.

Ralph Neighbour, of Touch Ministries, *describes a person's oikos as those to whom we devote some significant periods of time.* It is these persons who become part of our personal community. He believes most healthy people can identify about nine people in this way.[48] We make our most important and primary witness in our oikos! These are the non-church people we invite first. It's right here that searching people will look at *who we are* before they will listen to *what we say!* Just imagine the exponential possibilities. Bring one, and open the door to nine more!

Peter Wagner offers this simple formula: Celebration + Congregation + Cell =Church.[49] All the groups put together make up the congregation that assembles for joyous celebration. The whole is bigger than any of its parts, but all its parts are very important. *They interlock in a relational*

---

47   Peter C. Wagner, *Church Growth.* (Wheaton, IL: Tyndale House Publishers, 1988), 53.

48   Neighbour, *Where Do We Go From Here?*, 114.

49   Peter C. Wagner, Your Church Can Grow (Regal Books, CA 91209, 1976), 97 PAGE NUMBER(S).

way. In connection to their focus on the person of God the Father (Matt. 6:9), we realize that our own focus and identity is discovered in that sense of otherness. (That's why God made community in the beginning!) There is always something beyond us that helps us to realize identity.

That's the apostolic mind! In the following diagram, I have placed the foundations at the bottom and work upward. Of course, the *laos,* the people, are also very close to the entire foundation of the church, to Jesus Christ. We must remember that *in practice, this is a relational structure.* There is a good possibility that many New Testament churches organized themselves in ways something like this:

A Structure for a Group-Based Congregation

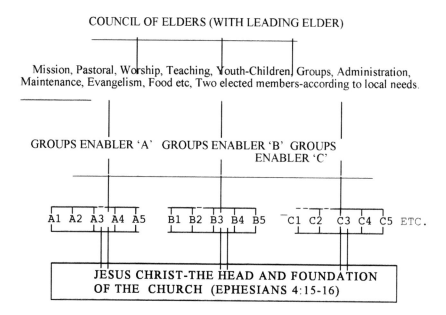

With church planting as a goal, the entire system of the congregation continues in a steady state of growth. We see how it remains apostolic and how it relates to a broader picture:

Pattern of a Church-Planting Congregation

1, 2, 3 ... 20   (Total of about 250 adults in one congregation attached to about twenty home groups.)

Multiple Congregations in One Church Fellowship. An overseer or system of oversight is required for this number of congregations.

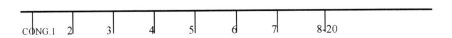

CONG.1 2 3 4 5 6 7 8-20

This schema is about churches who are committed to church-planting through personal evangelism. In order for it to remain relational, this structure begins again when a goal of 5,000 adults are aligned. (20 congregations of 250 adults).

Some Principles of a Relational Grouping of Churches

1. The primary principle revolves around relationships not territorial authority.

2. Every church community is connected to the nearest group of developing twenty churches. That sense of otherness is a catholicity of belonging to something other than, and bigger than, one community or group. This mind-set is an imperative adjunct to an apostolic mind-set.

3. As church planting increases, those groupings of twenty may change alignment. The larger and tighter the system grows the less territory will be required for most existing overseers. An overseer (or group) must be affirmed in gifts of encouragement and accountability. The overseer, or group of oversight, should also be accountable to the collective councils (or representatives) of the multiple congregations.

4. Each overseer will be based in one of the churches in which oversight is given. By limiting a group of churches to 5,000 adults, an overseer will also experience the joys and problems of a relational community.

5. None of the above principles are compromised when local

congregations are also in fellowship with nearby church groups (denominational or independent). These local churches come together for shared ministry, encouragement and accountability.

At the local level, we see quite easily that the aim is not to produce a mega-church. A major aim of the church is that it always *operates in a relational way*. The left hand does know what the right hand is doing. Therefore, when the numbers approach about 250 adults, plus young people, it is time to consider planting another church community.

Looking for an alternative, a group of young people kept asking me to lead them in developing a new church. I broke my own rule, and it proved to be disastrous. Many brought with them the egos and baggage of their former churches. The rule is this: *A church-plant is best when it is not a dissident or breakaway community but one that is seeded by a mature church.* In other words, a new church must be produced from a growing parent community. In this situation, *the parent church provides three mature core groups to begin the new work.* Less than that will mean problems in forging new directions and difficulties in abandoning old and unnecessary baggage. A lot of pioneering joy and support is lost in such a situation.

Who May Minister in a Group?

"I think my friend is ready to receive Jesus now." We were gathered in our home for our weekly meeting. Having finished my formal ministry at St. Mary's, Metchosin, Victoria, I was beginning to realize how much denominational baggage had influenced me. Incidentally, I am not against denominations. They provide great diversity in the wider church, *so long as there is a Christ-centered focus*. But now that I am away from it, I am also able to understand the weaknesses of a program-based church, with the amount of baggage that's required to support a large institution.

We had just stood around an elderly person who needed prayers for healing. Mrs. Cunningham was a lovely, arthritic lady who never thought she could ever make it to the group again. I couldn't carry her! When some of the young people heard why she wasn't there, they charged upstairs.

In ten minutes she was in our house, accompanied by the assurance she would be brought there every week. At the end of the evening, after we had prayed for her, she pushed her wheelchair back home! She was there every week, but she walked there! Her physical healing wasn't totally complete but considerably better. Imagine what that did for those young street people who had prayed for her!

Hannah had brought a seventeen-year-old street person. At this time, Hannah was nineteen years old. She had become really impressed by the power of the gospel in those real-life situations. She wanted me to lead her friend to Jesus. This Jesus was for real! I turned to Hannah and whispered, "I'm not going to do it. You lead her to Jesus."

"I've never done that," she blurted out in fear.

So as not to embarrass her, I continued to whisper, "You have seen how it's done right here. It's not your words that do the work; it's the Holy Spirit. Just introduce her to Jesus."

"How do I do that?" Hanna fearfully blurted out.

"Well, just tell her to tell Jesus that she is sorry for everything she has done wrong. Then she can thank Jesus for His forgiveness. Oh, and by the way, ask her to invite Jesus into her life. The rest is up to the Holy Spirit, not you or her."

She trusted me. "I'll give it a try," she replied.

Many of us gathered around the seventeen-year-old while Hannah asked her to repeat a simple prayer after her. It wasn't very sophisticated, but she remembered the basic things.

"I'm sorry, Jesus. Forgive me. Come into my heart. Thank you!"

And the Holy Spirit did the rest! The life of that girl was wonderfully changed. Hannah went on from these beginnings to a Christian university and has since graduated with a bachelor's degree! She now spends her life working as a social worker.

And where did she first learn how to minister? In a home group!

How Often Should Groups Meet?

Please allow me to repeat that home groups take place *twice a month*. On the other two weeks of the month, the church holds training and education courses. Remember that a major reason why we structure the group-based church in this way is because:

1. Jesus Christ is seen to be the Head and foundation of the entire church community. It enables an effective priesthood of believers.

2. Newcomers first meet a church community at a level that is comfortable to them.

3. The primary focus of the structure shows that it has outward priorities.

4. Throughout the entire system, the principle of ministry beyond is enabled by encouragement and accountability.

5. It provides a natural way for the development of church-planting.

6. With Jesus as the foundation, it cannot be a hierarchical structure.

7. The home group event is useful but not sufficient for training and teaching.

8. The agenda for ministry, education and training comes from the groups, not from people beyond.

Jesus Christ is the beginning, the end, the Head, and the very foundation of the Christian community and of all things (1 Cor.3:11; Col.1:17)! That puts Jesus beyond all fickleness, fads, and the evolving values of changing cultures.

> Jesus Christ is the same yesterday and today and forever.
> (Heb. 13:8)

We notice immediately, and in practice, that the direction, the agenda, and the structure of ministry *begin from the bottom upward. It is not hierarchical.* Clearly this event is different than most group situations.

A structure such as this reinforces the principle with which we began this book: *the gospel never changes, but its methodology must!*

Yet, this is a principle that propels us *back to the future.* Let me briefly explain the process of how this group-based church works: The foundation of everything is Jesus Christ. He is our bottom line. What this means is that everything emanating from Him takes on the very character and nature of Jesus. Everything is measured against His life and example. He is the foundation stone, the cornerstone, and the entire basis for a group-based church.

With basic foundations revolving around an intimate relationship with Jesus, and a conscious empowerment of the Holy Spirit, the natural question of the fellowship ceases to be, "What do I want for my church?" but it becomes, *"What does Jesus want for His church?"*

Clusters of Five Groups

The people of God (the laos) become the next stage in the process. It is these people who make possible all successive stages. (A Bible study group does not.) Of course, some leadership is required to initiate this primary stage. It would be disastrous to put people into groups without a competent leader of the group. In the Timothy Institute of Ministry, we have produced a PowerPoint presentation. It is a Saturday event (9:00 a.m. till 4:30 p.m.). The presentation informs the people of a congregation how the group-based system works. The presentation, entitled "Another Way," ably demonstrates why there must be another way and explains how the group-based church may well be an answer.

There is no point in holding this session unless:

1. The church council is present.

2. A very high percentage of the congregation is present.

3. At the final session, there must be a very high percentage of those present who vote to adopt this new system. Only after the congregation (or at least, the vast majority) has decided that they

want to move in this direction should a church even attempt to move on.

A positive decision will allow the pastor and/or other leaders to decide on how many groups and clusters will begin. That way it is easier to determine how many leaders are needed. Just because someone has previously been ministering as a Bible teacher doesn't necessarily qualify the person as a group enabler. This is definitely not the forum for someone who wants to be a Bible teacher. (Please take special note of the proceeding section on "Nine Reasons Why it Can Fail."). The most basic and minimum requirement is that a potential leader must have completed a *Growing in Christ* or an *Alpha* course. By now, the leader has realized the importance of putting everything to prayer. Some basic training on *how to facilitate groups* will come next. (Probably four or five sessions will do as a primer. See the Timothy Institute web page.) This is not a full-fledged course on group dynamics but simply a short course on *how to enable and facilitate a group*. If the pastor is not the best suited to facilitate this training, there is usually a social worker or some other professional in the church or local area. Incidentally, police, social workers and gifted teachers from other churches, will be very helpful resources in the education and training process of the church.

Core Groups

After this primary leadership course, it is important to form *core groups*. After many years of trying different ways, I discovered that it is important to let the chosen group leaders also choose about five other people to join them. They may be gleaned from a list of those desiring to join these special core groups. Of course, *these five people will be those who are already friends and who can relate at a deeper level to each other and the group leader.* After they have met by themselves for a few times, this group of six may then invite others *who do not already belong to the congregation ... Who do not ...!* This way, nothing can go wrong, can go wrong, can go ... (So it said on the record player!)

The group is the primary vehicle for evangelism. Those who are invited in are now able to see the *core group modeling all the purposes for the* group event. This core group may stay together indefinitely. *A maximum of twelve members is most strongly urged.* Once the group grows to be larger than this, the *quality of individual involvement* begins to diminish. It is at this point, or after no more than a year, that another core group of six from the twelve continues the process of multiplication growth. *Every group has a purpose designed to multiply itself. Every church has a purpose designed to church-plant another church.*

Purposes of a Home Group

1. *Evangelism*: The group-based church is more effective for bringing people and leading them to Christ, also for church-planting.

2. *Fellowship and Nurture*: For sharing and personal ministry.

3. *Ministry*: Each group ministers internally but also maintains an outward focus through one of the church's ministries.

What about Existing Church Ministries?

That brings me to a very important point. *What happens to all the existing programs now that the church has decided to become group-based?* You cannot have an existing program-church with a group-based church emerging alongside. *It just leads to competition, and neither will work properly.* I have tried it, and it failed! Most of those programs may already be effective and useful ministries. But all ministries are now focused in the church groups. No longer do we want ministries going on that are isolated from the larger vision of the whole body in that place. Later we will see that every home group has its own sense of ministry. *Indeed, much of the people resources for these existing ministries may be supplemented and encouraged by the groups.* In this way, the whole church is involved, and those who are ministering in these programs become encouraged and also accountable to the wider body. All of those existing ministries, approved by the groups as being part of the wider church vision, incorporate the ministries into the bigger, group-based vision.

The Enabler of Group Leaders

As we may have noticed, the home groups become the basis for developing the life of the entire congregation. But what they are discovering also needs facilitating throughout the entire system. Two words are clearly of vital importance. They are *encouragement and accountability—in that order!*

All the groups need leaders who have both of these gifts to enable their own ministry of leading a group. Who does this? The leading elder works with the council elder for groups. Probably that council member is one of the zone leaders (or enablers). A zone leader may also be a deacon who is responsible to meet regularly with five group leaders (he or she may be one of them). A group enabler may well be a deacon or an existing small group leader. At this regular meeting, there are five group leaders who meet *no less than once every three months*. In calling to account what has been going on in the groups represented, the enabler does not do so in judgment but in encouragement. I have learned that when the purposes of the groups are not moving forward, *it is almost always because these meetings have lapsed. We may easily see that a group enabler is a key position for the life of the entire church and that the entire church system is relational.*

At this meeting, the enabler hears the problems and joys going on in the groups. Joys and problems, shared together, relieve burdens on group leaders and also on clergy. The zone leader will also hear common problems arising in all the basic group meetings. In the meetings with group leaders, the enabler gleans what the groups need in the way of education or training. In this way, the council will be informed, and the gifted elders will become involved. It is also in this way the needs of the church and its ministries emerge—*not from the top down but from the bottom up.* Here is a short list of some topics that do emerge from the groups:

1. Raising teenagers

2. Managing finances

3. Dealing with stress in the workplace

4. Running a soup or food kitchen

5. Understanding the major needs of the local community

6. Family life

7. Learning how to ask questions in the group

8. Understanding the Bible

9. How to listen to those with problems

10. Principles of leadership

11. Training for church ministries

12. How to minister in the Spirit

13. The need for special Bible courses

14. Communication problems in the groups

It is not difficult to see that the process of discipleship goes on in a continual manner. Incidentally, the reason for such a priority of thought is that most of the group members may not be seasoned churchgoers, yet all of its members have personal questions, needs, and areas of growth. The group is to be the very backbone of discipleship, so the process of education and training begins with the groups.

I must stress how important the groups may be in training for ministry. The initial core groups are more likely to be more mature in exercising their own ministries. Those who are added to the group see real people sharing their problems and then how the problems are addressed in a relational manner. They also see ordinary people sharing *revelations* and leading people to Christ.

The relationship of group enablers to group leaders may be summed up like this:

1. To *encourage* five group leaders in their problems and joys.

2. To call into *account* the goals and purposes of each group.

3. To call for accountability in *facilitating the wider purposes of the*

congregation. Hence, the enabler helps group leaders to focus beyond the immediate life of the group.

4. To *encourage and pray* with those *five group leaders* for their group goals and individual concerns.

The Council of Elders

Of course, the number of elders depends upon the size of the congregation and the number of spiritually-gifted leaders. However, a major problem in most churches is that the decision-makers are *elected* on to the council. Here is a church that is following a secular, institutional pattern. Whether these elected people know much about the problems they encounter is often debatable. It is highly likely that they are making decisions in areas for which they are most definitely not gifted. Was it always like this?

As we have noticed previously, people who were spiritually gifted in particular areas occupied positions or offices in the first-century church. Titles were of a spiritual, not an institutional, nature. *A church that offers training in ministry also honors regular use of spiritual gifts inventories.* Consequently the group enablers are informed of the gifts exercised in the groups. The method provides a forum of good communication.

Clearly, Paul is instructing Titus concerning what to do to begin organizing the churches in orderly ways. From that time on, the decisions had to come from within the local churches, at least with regard to *who* the decision-makers should be. They will be the spiritually gifted church elders who represent a variety of gifts. It is these people who are fully responsible to promote ministries within their charge. Yet the entire group of elders will be fully aware and careful of the progress of those ministries. In this way, the entire life of the local church is brought to the attention of the elders.

Paradoxically, I can remember times when people would address me at St. James with a puzzled comment, "You don't seem to know half of what is going on in this church, do you?" I would reply, "You're right! I don't know, and I don't want to know." They didn't know they were complimenting me.

Actually, at our meetings of commission heads (from a wider

institutional perspective, we could not call them elders), leaders became quite well informed of each other's progress and problems. *However, we made it a point to give full responsibility to the elder responsible for that ministry.* If they had to clear everything with me first, then how could the leaders grow? If I jumped in to make decisions when they had problems, how could they learn? (And that also assumes I am gifted for making those decisions.) Communication and prayer were very important at our times of meeting. We got to know each other as real people, with both joys and problems. We had fun together. And we got beyond the usual treasurer's question, "Can we afford to do this ministry?" It was a question that was very rarely asked. The first and most important question was, "What does Jesus want in this situation?"

Questions of volunteers to take over vacant ministries no longer emerged. Each elder was responsible to ensure future leadership was being raised up from within that commission. (Each elder had supporting committee members to ensure that the work was being done.)

In reality, I can't recall even one elder who refused to discuss ministry problems and joys with me. If each felt a need to go beyond the council meetings, *they were always great opportunities for sharing and for prayer.* I have also come to feel that elders should be given a long term in office. Maybe each church has to experiment with this question. After that, the council and leading elder decide on renewing the term. The elder may also request the extension. Certain elders may feel called, with the approval of council, to hold that position in perpetuity. For the sake of the kingdom, what does Jesus want? That's the question. For the sake of further communication between the council and church members, a couple of people (not as elders) should also be elected from the church membership. A two-year term would suffice.

The Leading Elder

As we saw in the relation of Peter to the other eleven apostles, he was usually the spokesperson for the group but not the sole decision-maker (Acts 15:19, 22). Often contact with a local church is best achieved through one person rather than one group. In normal situations, it would be preferable if the person were ordained and ordination was recognized by a larger body (such as *a major denomination* or *a fellowship of apostolic, first-century churches, which could present its own standards*). Here, we note that the process toward ordination may not always be via a standard number of years in or out of a college residence.

The entire principle of training for ordination must come under scrutiny. Who said candidates need to accumulate massive amounts of money to pay for years of hiding behind the walls of those hallowed halls? *Why should not the teachers of higher education come to them as selected groups?* Teachers also need to have hands-on learning from the church in action. And in the group-based church, ample opportunity may well be given for hands-on training and special education for special purposes in ministry (e.g., the alternative education night to the group event). Provision could also be made for seminary teachers to tutor those moving toward ordination. Imagine teachers meeting regularly with potential ordinands from a number of churches. Imagine this connection being made through the internet. Much of this work could also be done by correspondence *while candidates are still in the field of church ministry.* Nowadays, the internet has already proven to be a powerful medium in facilitating this purpose. I, like many others, became isolated from the real world of ministry for many years and at considerable expense. We can see how this leading elder might receive formal recognition from a wider church community than is needed for the local church.

The leading elder will in all probability hold one of the ministries given to elders. That ministry might well be one of worship, teaching, pastoral ministry, or any area in which the leading elder is spiritually gifted. Probably, in what will mostly be a full-time position, this person will also be responsible to facilitate church-planting from among the membership and ensure a potential leader has received adequate training. Gifted people in leadership may well continue an education process through established colleges or universities.

The leading elder will also be responsible to look beyond the local situation, and to enable the possibility of inter-church ministries in the local area. *This is a vital ministry to churches that realize that no church, in any given area, has all the resources needed to minister effectively in that situation alone!* And this may well be the forum for some of the church groups to exercise and share ministry and resources with other churches. Depending upon the situation, the picture, in a given area, may look something like this:

Outreach Ministry

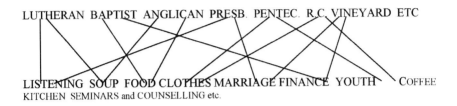

LUTHERAN BAPTIST ANGLICAN PRESB. PENTEC. R.C. VINEYARD ETC

LISTENING SOUP FOOD CLOTHES MARRIAGE FINANCE YOUTH COFFEE
KITCHEN SEMINARS and COUNSELLING etc.

We see how unity of ministry concerns in a given region will draw attention to the church but not to a particular denomination! Does all of the above hang on the effectiveness of the home group? Yes, it does! Much too many churches with home groups occupy their time in Bible study. Bible study is vitally important, at a different level than the home group. It is not the most effective manner in which small groups should spend their time. *We will look at a better way.*

CHAPTER 10

The Big Event—What Really Works?

This entire biblical system hinges on the quality of what happens during those two *big event* sessions of each month. *If this fails, everything fails!* If it is done well, you are going to find an eager church. It will be a church possessing a powerful apostolic, caring, ministering, growing, and relational character that would be the pride of all first-century Believers. Believe it or not, all I have said previously is totally dependent upon *what happens at the group event.* A Bible study group cannot possibly achieve all that has been outlined in this book. Here is the process for the group session. Apart from a flexibility of time used for each segment, *this form is not a suggestion* but an *essential* in achieving the above apostolic goals. It is also a wonderful method in which churches may keep their members in a growing process of discipleship.

Who Is Invited to the Group?

Once I had become totally comfortable concerning the effectiveness of the home-based church, I realized something of its admission rules. *There aren't any!* At least there are no rules concerning who may be invited. Remember, this is probably the most meaningful experience of being *included that many have ever known in their entire lives.* Every member of a core group passes on to newcomers the importance of continually inviting others.

If two men are sitting there hand in hand and they don't come back next time, where does the problem lay? If there's a businessman who is known to behave unjustly with his employees and who also doesn't come back, where does the problem lay? If there's a man and woman who live together and who fail to show up next time, where is the problem? How can we minister to people when we push them away? However, we really must make some important *distinctions* here.

Imagine bringing to church a twenty-year-old young lady with rings in her nose, green hair, and boots up to her chin. That was Hannah! Imagine bringing to church a twenty-five-year-old, 220-pound ex-convict who has a clean-shaven head and tattoos down to his toes. Imagine bringing an ex-con who hasn't lost the ability or desire to relieve your group members of the burden of their money. Imagine bringing a thirty-two-year-old who has spent sixteen years of his life behind bars. Imagine bringing a young junkie who says he is now a Christian but shot-up on cocaine twenty minutes before he arrived! And imagine bringing nice church people (from an entirely different world) because they think the experience can mean something more to their lives and their families. Maybe they could also learn something from those strange people from La-La Land!

These are not people arising from my imagination. We had them all in our house because they couldn't feel easy, welcome, or accepted in a church. If you have an unmarried couple who live together, they're welcome! If you have a person who has given up on the church, he or she is welcome! (We are likely to see many today who have given up on the church *but not on Jesus*. It may be that the church has been a cause for their hurt. We cannot be the cause of such hurt again!) If you have an alcoholic who fell off the wagon *after joining the church*, he's still welcome! If you have a straight-laced church person, he's welcome too, provided he sees himself as a learner among learners. *All of these scenarios I have just presented are* not fictitious; I have experienced all of them in home situations. Most of those people I describe really did find their way to our house! And all of them came back. We must introduce a rider here:

Most of those people are not ready for leadership in the church!

Nor will their training for leadership be acceptable to the community until they have embarked on the new life in Christ through repentance. But prior to this, their preparation has to begin with an open-hearted acceptance of them as people who need Jesus and with our unreserved friendship. *The gospel is for the "whosoever" (John 3:16). However, the qualifications for leadership in the church are not for those who want the gospel on their own terms (Matt. 22:1–14) or for those who haven't participated in leadership and discipleship training (Eph. 4:12–13).*

The group event should most definitely not last more than two hours. We must remember our promise to participants; it will not go on all night. Some of them may be paying for babysitters, and it is not fair to them. That is, especially if the length has got out of hand because of *sloppiness in leadership.* However, on occasion, there may well be a reason to keep on ministering to someone. In such a situation, the leader must end on time with a prayer. Those who need to leave are allowed to go. Others may want to stay behind to help in ministry. Always keep in mind that we should not play on the goodness of those who have hosted the event.

There are roughly three sections comprising the entire group occasion:

1. Individual ministry in the Spirit

2. Bible application

3. Vision for ministry and thanksgivings

Here is a diagram of how the event would go:

AN ORDER FOR A GROUP SESSION

	SUGGESTED TIMES
1. INTRODUCTION OF GUESTS- INFORMAL TIME	10
2. SHORT OPENING PRAYER	
3. ICE-BREAKER OR PRAISE SINGING-If and when appropriate.	10
4. QUESTIONS TO GROUP: (1)WHAT HAVE YOU BEEN FINDING DIFFICULT IN YOUR LIFE LATELY? (2) IN WHAT WAYS MAY WE HELP?	30-35

These questions may be followed by ministry of prayer and practical sharing of how the group may offer or find help.

5. SHORT REFRESHMENT BREAK	10
6. BIBLE APPLICATION -on practical issues of life, or questions that have arisen from the group	30-35
7. VISION: How are we meeting our ministry goals in the group?	15
8. QUESTION (3) What are the good things for which we want to thank God?	10

9. CLOSING PRAYERS of THANKSGIVING

TWO HOURS MAXIMUM

Section 1 (Individual Ministry in the Spirit)

The core groups hold the first couple of sessions alone—in other words, before guests are invited. Therefore, there will be little problem becoming acquainted with each other. However, an opening time of informality should precede the session. Football or hockey scores may be appropriate. Someone will open with a *short prayer*. Later, invited guests will be put off by a long prayer. A short time of praise singing may follow, provided all members are familiar with or are provided with words for the songs.

With this core group, maybe only one person will initially respond to the opening question. That's all right, because no one should feel pressured to participate. It won't take long before this session becomes a very powerful juncture of sharing. This is not the time for advice-givers to take over. The power will be in prayer and caring. Some very practical contributions may be made here. That will be seen especially as the second question is asked. One person may suggest having coffee with the troubled person. Another may suggest a helpful resource. However, everyone may gather around the person who sits in the middle. *Everyone who prays lays hands on the person in the chair.*

A number of prayers may be made, but this is also an opportunity for *revelations of the Spirit*. Words of knowledge or prophecy may follow. There may be tongues and an interpretation. (*Obviously, in this situation, all the core group members have completed something like the Growing in Christ course.*) Imagine how guests may feel when it is clear the Spirit has been present and the revelation is clearly shown to be true. Mature Christians often surprise guests who see that mature people have problems, like themselves, and that the Holy Spirit cares and operates through ordinary people. *That's the way it worked in the first-century church* (Acts 8:12–13).

This time of ministry can be quite exhausting. It is therefore very appropriate to have a refreshment break. It is just ten minutes for a couple of important reasons. First of all, this time can devolve into a long and fruitless chat. Second, this is not a time to cause competition among those who bring the refreshments. It becomes a big deal, and often threatening to someone else. Coffee or tea with some biscuits (cookies) on hand is quite sufficient. In some churches, the hosts are relieved from contributing to this further task.

Section 2 (Bible Application)

The group is the primary instrument of evangelism. Therefore, the Bible appears before people who won't know where on earth to find the book of Deuteronomy. They won't know who the patriarchs are. They won't know the difference between the Old and the New Testaments. But they do need to know that the Bible actually speaks to their life situations. They will fall in love with it if they are introduced to it in this way. This problem of a people without a religious memory is becoming more and more the norm.

I will always be grateful to Cliff Bentham. He was a truck driver with a passion for evangelism. Often, he would bring street people to our home church in Victoria. I thought it would be a good idea, at the beginning, to do a study on Philippians. It wasn't!

"Charles, you are leaving these street people way behind you. They need to hear something that applies to their own lives."

I was stumped. There had to be a better way, but how could it be done?

Prayer!

After a lot of it, God showed me how to proceed for the next week. The session was to be all about Bible application. But it had to be at a place in which all the people could identify. It would be connected with the ministry that had gone before.

Please, please, please don't let it devolve into a Bible study. Don't let the leader be a Bible teacher. There's a place for that; it may be at next week's education session. I will guarantee that, if this session becomes a Bible study, the outward focus will disappear (and so will some of the guests). I know that, where this has happened, the group rarely changes. I know of one group where it never changed in fifteen years. The members were happy, but I wonder how many people were never given an opportunity to begin a new life in Jesus Christ.

The very next week, we had our time of ministry and a coffee break. Then we sat down for Bible application. It was stunning the way the street people were involved. I picked up on a common aspect of our ministry time: depression. Then I asked everyone to listen to a passage from 1 Kings 19. It was all about how depressed Elijah felt after Jezebel had chased him out of town. The Word came alive for everyone there, and it proved to be powerful for those to whom we had ministered.

Now this doesn't mean we should expect that a leader would know where to find a particular subject in the Bible. (There are aids these days.) To compensate for this, sometimes I would ask the group if anyone recalled a passage of Scripture that was useful when going through a problem. All the core group Christians could pick up on this invitation. They would share how a passage of Scripture had been helpful. It was amazing what this did for the ex-convicts and street people.

"The Bible really speaks to problems like mine!"

"These Christians have problems too."

I cannot ever remember a dull Bible application time. The involvement was amazing! We were meeting people where they were; we were ministering to each other where people were feeling pain. But our aim was not to leave them there!

Section 3 (Vision for Ministry and Thanksgivings)

This section is primarily designed to make certain each individual group possesses an *outward focus*. We have already noted how easy it is for a group to develop a primary *inward focus*. It's amazing how guests can contribute to ministries that are needed. Initially ministries throughout the groups will be already-existing ministries that are now focused on the groups for support.

Of course, at the beginning, these goals may not have been determined, but it does help us to consider the need to do some *transitioning here*. To this point, your church may have been a program church, even if it incorporated home groups. That doesn't mean those programs were not useful. Indeed, it may be a tragedy to drop some of them. The church that has decided to become group-based knows full well that *good programs also need to be incorporated into the group system*. Others ministries may well be done better by using the resources of the church groups. For example, we don't want to honor the old style of Bible study and especially with someone who wants to be a Bible teacher. *The next week (the alternate week)* a very good teacher may well be addressing that situation.

Groups that have formerly operated in that way will come under the group-based system with a leader who is qualified to be a small group enabler. If that group, or any other kind of group, keeps on going the same way, then the church is destined to spend years awaiting the result of a *competition* between the group-based church and the program-based church. Nothing fares well, at least in terms of the church purposes.

It is here that the groups (as they vision) are able to move toward ministries that better fit the larger goals of the church. For example, if the congregation has been called to feed the poor, then the people resources are found in a group, or several groups, that have felt called to minister in that direction. It may well be that a group may have several people who are gifted, or who have a passion, in another area. The group may well be comprised of people engaged in two areas of ministry. In my last church of enabling, one group consisted of the music ministry. A single focus like that is also helpful in aiding people to work out their time priorities.

At the group's vision session, these directions will be determined in prayer. Later, as reports are being shared, the leader gleans the joys, problems, and needs to be more effective. It is also at this time that the group will *share the difficulties and the joys of inviting new people to join them.* This should happen very frequently. At his or her meeting with the group enabler (zone leader), these insights will be shared, and the council will receive a broader picture of what ministries are being done throughout the group-based church. *The group enabler will also be helpful in bringing the right resources together.*

In my early days of experimentation, I felt that the group event should start off with a bang before it got into ministry, so the session really began with thanksgivings. Unfortunately, that left personal ministry to the end of the session. Some people went home with their legs dragging behind them. It is much better to deal with heaviness much earlier on. After vision and goal sharing, it is very powerful and joyful to end the session with thanksgiving.

Imagine the reaction of guests when they hear real-life stories of what God has been doing. This God is alive! And so are the people in the group! Before a closing prayer, what a powerful and joyous way this is to end the entire session.

Nine Reasons Why It Can Fail

After many years of personal discovery and experimentation, I have found out what is really powerful and effective. I also learned why the group-based church is the most exciting way to do ministry and enable discipleship. But that process has also taught me about the things that cause failure. This whole thing is much too important and wonderful for me to stop here. Here are nine reasons that I have discovered that contribute to a waste of time and effort:

1. Pastors: For over eighteen hundred years, there has grown a co-dependency between pastors and people of a congregation. The pastor (a term never used in the New Testament as the ministry of one person) does most of the ministry. He or she meets the spiritual needs of all the people, and he can expect the church to support him in his material needs. This very unbiblical (but

institutional) approach has led to wrong expectations. *The pastor has been expected to enable and control all ministries,* and all church ministry also has to go through him first. If he gives the required support, then people think it is bound to work. *This has to end! When the pastor is controlling the development of the group-church, it is doomed from the beginning.* As we have seen, the congregation is allowed to make the initial decision, and it will be in the congregation that vision for continuous development, ministry, and growth will emerge. Even if the pastor means well, please don't let him dictate the course of events. *In other words, stop him from doing traditional things (not traditional enough) where gifted people are being excluded from leadership and decision-making.* The spiritually gifted pastor is a *gift from God.* He will be the one who actually enables this process honoring the vision and ministry of the priesthood of all believers (1 Pet. 2:9).

2. Program-church competition: Once there is competition between existing programs and the group-based Church, you are destined for years of ineffective struggle. The congregation must be given an informed idea of this new possibility. (See PowerPoint presentation from the Timothy Institute of Ministry.) The group-based process (when given freedom to move) affects the entire life of the congregation. One program doesn't. But it can get in the way if it is not incorporated into the group system. Existing ministries must be incorporated into the goals, the enabling, the accountability, and the encouragement of groups. In this way, *the entire church becomes accountable, relational, and supportive.*

3. When the third section of the group event (visioning) is ignored or not properly done, the *outward focus of the groups* will begin to diminish. Indeed, the process requires that all three sections be addressed at every group event.

4. In each section, when the process of *accountability and encouragement* becomes weak, there is no way to know where

the weaknesses are and how to remedy them. It is easy to lapse into an event that is comfortable but no longer productive.

5. The decision-makers on the council and the leading elder should be spiritually gifted for their own particular areas of leadership. One portfolio is all that one elder can handle, and that is also true for the leading elder. It is better for a church to refuse to meet a need when the resources are not in place. Otherwise, the ministry may be done badly, and someone may be hurt.

6. Group leaders should not be chosen from those who want to be teachers. Leaders need to be trained to be enablers. Otherwise, the event will easily devolve into a Bible study and thus defeat the bigger purposes. Bible application has much better effect.

7. A comfortable coziness may easily develop in a group, but it should never hinder the release of another core group that has developed from within. The unwillingness to produce and release another core group hinders natural growth. (Up to a year of developing and modeling is recommended. Earlier release than this may easily cause discouragement and just at points where the group feels it is progressing.)

8. A church plant should never be a breakaway or disgruntled community. Each new group expression should be seeded and encouraged by a parent body. Otherwise, the new core group will take with it all the baggage it never previously handled.

9. Once there is a *breakdown of regular meetings between group leaders and group enablers*, the entire system has entered into a process of erosion and self-destruction. The oversight of the leading elder is very helpful here. Encouragement and accountability are sorely needed. Without this vital form of communication it is very easy for prayers to emerge that omit the question, What do you want Lord Jesus; what has all this to do with the kingdom of God.

It Sounds Too Big and Complicated for Us

That's a very good point, and it's especially true when we realize that (in mainline churches), an average congregation numbers about seventy. In Canada, it is even less. *Actually, it is not a problem.*

We begin where we are. Once a church has done some basics of discipleship and *through a lot of prayer*, has determined to move forward, even a small church is able to start moving with *three or four core groups*. (That's also the point where a new church-plant may begin.) Anything less than three or four groups means the church is not yet ready to start in new directions. I have always operated under the principle that *you can only go with those who will go!*

If a church has come to the point where the large majority has agreed to go in a group-based direction, then the leadership must be prepared to move and leave behind those who will not go.

That sounds like an awful thing to say to a leader who has a pastoral heart. Not even Jesus kept the original twelve. The fact is, if the congregation has arrived at this decision in consensus and concerted prayer, then a few people (who may well have good reason not to be able to join a group) cannot expect to control the movement of those who will go where God is leading. Of course, we really have assumed that much fervent prayer has gone into this decision. The fact is, those who cannot move forward will never be deprived of love and acceptance. They are always welcome to remain with the congregation at their own level. *However, they will not be allowed to impede the growth of those who will move on.* Yes, the entire system gets scaled down to what is feasible for three or four groups. However, the old forms of determining leadership will no longer apply.

Conclusion

Verna and I started off this quest with more than a yearlong journey. Of course, we knew from the very beginning that we would never find a perfect church, but we were looking for a church that had credibility in first-century principles. In the search, we were beginning to realize how many churches had settled into traditions of their own making. Actually, we never did discover even one church, and certainly not a denomination, that had willingly embraced the challenge. *But then, it had also taken me some years to realize how much I viewed the kingdom of God through the filters of my own denomination.* Of course, people of other churches were doing the same thing.

Even when I asked pastors of mainline evangelical churches if they considered themselves to be biblically based, they would answer in surprised amazement, "Of course we are." We realize they were also speaking through old filters laden with dust. There was a need for clean and effective filters to examine the efficiency of *structures, worship, and apostolic witness.* If this sounds daunting to some, it is important to remember *we will never find a perfect church anywhere.* The second thing is this: We must be rooted in the body of Christ somewhere. Gypsy-Christianity does almost nothing for our growth in Christ.

Many churches liked the idea of groups. They had become fashionable. But they had not carefully examined them for their historical value of facilitating three major avenues of kingdom life. In that light, I realized that, with all my good and bad experiences of the group-based church, this was the most effective way to restore first-century principles into the contemporary scene. It requires an unhindered screening, some considerable creativity, plus a lot of hard work and training by all church members (including the clergy) and at least informed growth in all those who take discipleship seriously.

No, we never did find one church or any denomination that came near meeting this standard. But the first-century church was not primitive. Certainly, from an institutional point of view, it wasn't sophisticated. However, unlike most of the sophisticated churches of today, it possessed all the principles, talent, focus, Spirit anointing, and diversity to be thoroughly apostolic. With slightly lowered expectations, Verna and I have a different project before us: *Instead of continuing the fruitless task of finding a church or a denomination that meets these criteria, we will begin looking for a church that is genuinely willing to risk the work of asking the Spirit to reform the clogged-up filters of their present existence.*

Will we be successful?

APPENDIX 1

Fellowship of Apostolic, First-Century Churches Statement of Purpose, Principles and Goals.

Purpose: This is not a denomination but a fellowship of denominational and independent churches. We do not desire to restore the first century into the present but to recover its essential apostolic principles as the basis for entering this Second Reformation. Therefore, in local situations, we come together as a fellowship of churches committed to mutual accountability, mission and encouragement. We do so on the basis of the historic, unchanging gospel of Jesus Christ (Heb. 13:8). This gospel, for all ages, is expressed in catholic (universal body), charismatic, and evangelical life. We recognize that the gospel of Jesus Christ never changes, but its methodology must (1 Thess. 5:21, Phil. 3:13). Therefore, in this present, pluralistic climate, we are not ashamed to declare that Jesus Christ is the Way, the Truth, and the Life for all peoples of all ages (John 14:6).

Goals: As in the first-century church, the methods, form, and structures conveying our witness are always diverse and flexible to demonstrate that the good news of Jesus is applicable to all times and in all cultures. We believe that our changing methods and forms will maintain gospel integrity by our unwavering commitment to the recovery of essential apostolic principles, as found in the first-century church:

1. **The Recovery of Apostolic Belief**

   Our God eternally exists in Trinity of persons: Father, Son, and Holy Spirit. It is the nature of God that determines the way we worship and minister in a broken and lost world. In our commitment to this historic faith, we honor leadership that is willing and capable of "contending for the faith once delivered to the saints" (Jude 3). To that end, we uphold the authority of the Bible and the agreed ecumenical creeds of the early church (i.e., the Apostles' Creed and the Nicene Creed).

2. **The Recovery Of An Apostolic Heart**

   Out of love for Christ and its response to the Great Commission (Matt. 28:19–20), people of the first-century church had a heart and passion for the lost. The church believed, uncompromisingly, that the salvation of Jesus Christ was for all people, of all times, and in all places (John 3:16). Phenomenal growth was apparent in its primary focus on planting new church communities. The first-century church was not embarrassed to put kingdom imperatives first (Matt. 6:33).

3. **The Recovery of Apostolic Praxis**

   In its praxis (what they did), the primitive church knew it could "do nothing" (John 15:5) apart from the anointing power of the Holy Spirit, as promised by Jesus (Luke 24:49). They were a community of Word and Spirit; what they said, they did (2 Cor.12:12). The prophetic word, plus signs and wonders, are encouraged in all who are recognized church leaders and members of this fellowship. They were also a community of Word and sacrament (signs of spiritual realities) (Acts 2:42, 1 Cor. 11:23–26). Therefore, this fellowship upholds the two gospel covenants of baptism and Holy Communion as expressions of the awesome mystery in which God promises to meet with us, through adoption into His family (John 1:12–13) and by His continual feeding of His body in the life of Christ.

4. **The Recovery of Apostolic Direction:**

The Greek word *apostello* means to be sent out. The apostolic focus is primarily outward, not inward. The church exists for the sake of others. A healthy church majors on activity beyond its walls by reaching out in love and justice to the hurting, the broken, and the lost (Matt. 25:45). The distribution of our individual church finances is an indication of outward focus.

5. **The Recovery Of Apostolic Nature**

It is servant-relational! Jesus Christ, the Head of the church (Eph. 1:22–23), washed the feet of His own disciples (John 13:12–14). In following the example of its Lord, the first-century church was not hierarchical (Matt. 20:25–28) but sought to serve in relational ways. The integrity of its relational structures honored the heart and nature of its Lord. Its approach to evangelism was always by way of invitation and never by compulsion. Its leaders possessed an authority that was exercised in servant-encouragement and accountability, not power-wielding autocracy.

6. **The Recovery of Apostolic Diversity**

Diversity without agreed focus is chaos. All gifts of ministry are focused in Christ as Head and are expressed according to His will and purpose (e.g., Eph. 4:11–13). Prior to the monochromatic structure of the church, such as that which had emerged in the third century, we note that there was no uniform structure in apostolic times. It seems that there was a principle uniquely questioned: "What form best demonstrates the unchanging gospel in ever-varying cultures?" Therefore, the church in Antioch was not structured in exactly the same way as the church in Jerusalem or Ephesus. By accepting the importance of accountability and encouragement, and also by maintaining sensitivity to changing culture, this fellowship honors oversight in a variety of forms upholding these apostolic principles.

In these days of Second Reformation, we believe that individual churches of this fellowship may express worship and service in the following ways:

1. Individually, local member churches will meet for worship around the table of the Lord's Supper at least two Sundays in each month. A flexible service will embrace a liturgical and/or a free form.

2. Both churches that worship liturgically and those of a free form, will allow for the offering of spiritual gifting by the worshippers. The goal in worship will be to encourage worshippers to have an intimate relationship with God in a sense of holy awe and wonder.

3. Nearby church representatives of the fellowship will meet on a

regular basis to offer mutual encouragement and accountability and will seek to share gifts for vital ministries in the local area.

4. The apostolic desire of the fellowship is to plant new communities of the faith that are built upon the life of new converts to Christ.

New or existing communities that seek to relate to the above methods of discipleship are welcome to connect with each other through the following ways:

Membership is confined to church communities that will actively agree to honor these goals, purposes, and principles and will demonstrate their desire to grow in such a process of fellowship.

Associate membership for church communities that are interested in becoming involved but need more time to think, pray, or work toward a decision regarding affiliation:

Please contact nearby churches to begin such a fellowship.

APPENDIX 2

House Churches And Home Groups

The house church cannot be ignored in the contemporary world. For example, the rapidly expanding church in China is largely attributable to the outlawed house churches. Similar growth amid a declining, institution-focused church community may be recognized in other places, such as in Britain. It's very necessary to recognize what was and what can be was.

After all, for at least 200 years the church (i.e., the ekklesia-the called out ones) met in houses, not in designated places built for worship. A church is a community, not a building. Nevertheless, we must recognize that places of worship have been, and can be very important for the present. Not only are church buildings designed to give a sense of awe and symbol, but have traditionally been the center of community activity and ministry in both rural and urban situations. In good stewardship, effective use of church buildings is still important-so long as they don't necessitate dragging along ineffective, traditional baggage. Or divert attention from our real focus of worship.

Constantine, through the Edict of Milan (AD313), not only made Christianity a legal religion, but also helped to model much of what was common to the norm of pagan religions as a norm for the church. The slow growing use of church buildings (from about AD 250) rapidly accelerated during his reign. They were named after great saints, just as pagan temples were formerly named after various pagan deities. Instead of God being wherever saints of God were assembled (Matt.28:20), God's Presence was sometimes thought to be located in 'holy' buildings. It is a highly debatable matter whether or not Constantine was good for the kingdom of God! He was certainly good for the church as a recognizable, and easily manageable institution within a geo-political and religious society. Can we learn something from early beginnings?

The merging of house churches with group-based communities. I see no reason why such a merger should not be highly effective in our contemporary world. Goals and purposes of a house church would be similar or the same as the group-based church.
Primarily, the house church sees itself as having an *outward focus* with an object of becoming a church-planting community. The primary methodology being by bringing people to Christ; not trying to fill pews. That's how the apostolic church grew.

Secondly, I believe members could also meet midweek for a group event, as suggested in chapter 10 while, on alternate weeks there would be an emphasis on training and further education (as suggested in this book). On the weekend all meet together for the specific purpose of communal worship. An outward focus will enhance the catholic sense of *belonging to the whole body of Christ*. The form of worship (mentioned in chapter 8) may be helpful in encouraging participation, spiritual gifting, and the releasing of the Holy Spirit in the gathering around the Lord's table.

Outward Focus: Titus 1:5, having travelled the Isle of Crete, I suspect, quite strongly, that the growing church there developed in a manner such as this: Possessing a primary outward focus, the goal was that every member witnessed the salvation of Jesus to those people who are normally close to them, (their oikos). I imagine a small group in every town grew to a house church of about 50 or maybe more. In the context we mention here, I would see that, at this point, one or two groups (of about 6-forming two new core groups) would be released to become the beginning of another house church. In that way, the primary goals of the old and new group remains fresh and foremost.

Worship: Of course, all the groups meet together in a house, or similar situation. It is important to remember that worship is not geared for seekers, but mature Christians, and those who have been invited from home groups to attend. A service, such as that outlined in chapter 8 recaptures something of the form, spiritual gifts, mystery-awe, and every-member participation, such as is evident in New Testament times. These principles are in direct contrast to the passively lay approach that is commonly experienced in too many churches of today. In this way, the entire goal of worship and discipleship is accomplished.

PREVIEW

*I*s your church among the vast majority ignoring most first-century principles? How does your church make disciples and keep on going? Where will it be ten years from now? Do you know what a group-based church is, which many churches think they are? Why is it the best way to keep churches growing? Do you want your church to be excited concerning the future? Loaded with personal examples of success and failure, *The Church I Couldn't Find* shows how churches of today can be very exciting and bursting with the Holy Spirit's life in the priesthood of all believers.

CPSIA information can be obtained at www.ICGtesting.com
Printed in the USA
LVOW12s1747240813

349392LV00004B/15/P

9 781449 789435